W9-ARX-627

Harvest mice live in tall grass and reeds. They are so light the grasses support their weight, and they can travel rapidly through long runways, seldom coming into the open.

THE GOLDEN BOOK OF
Animal Habits

This Book Belongs to:
Johnny Harsh
R3 Box 234 Eagle Lake
Edwardsburg Michigan

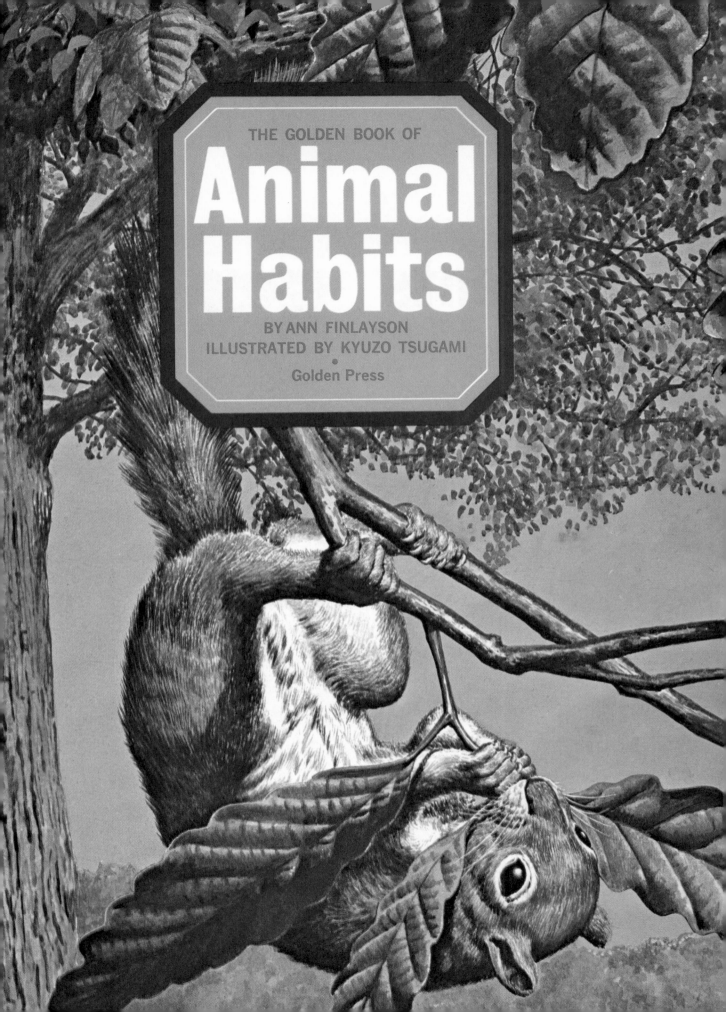

THE GOLDEN BOOK OF

Animal Habits

BY ANN FINLAYSON
ILLUSTRATED BY KYUZO TSUGAMI
•
Golden Press

Contents

Prepared and produced by
Rutledge Books, Inc.
Printed in the United States of America
by Western Printing and
Lithographing Company.
Published by Golden Press, Inc.
850 Third Avenue, New York, New York.
© 1965 by Golden Press, Inc.
Library of Congress Catalog
Card Number: 65-13497

A mother seal must urge her playful cubs to go into the water for their first lesson in swimming.

THE
ANIMAL KINGDOM
a world of
many wonders

The Golden Book of Animal Habits is a book that tells how animals sleep, keep house, live together, "talk" to each other, fight their enemies. It tells how they build their houses, find and eat their food, how they bring up their children, how they play.

Animals share with human beings the abilities to smell, hear, feel and taste. These senses are more highly developed in some animals than they are in people. They warn against danger; they signal that food is at hand. In the spring, they guide an animal to a mate.

Like people, animals find or build homes suited to their needs. Some require no more than the shade of a tree. Some take shelter only in severe weather, others when they want a home for their young.

Home can be a nest, a pile of leaves, an underground tunnel. Home can be a hole—in a tree, in a stump, in a stone wall. Generally, the homes are arranged strictly for comfort, not beauty. But one animal, the wood rat, decorates his house with something bright or glittery—a button, a piece of glass— that he has picked up on his travels.

Of course, animals and people have their own ways of doing things. Yet both animals and humans have needs and abilities and ambitions that are quite similar.

Some animals—probably more than we know about— can "talk" to each other. This isn't to say that they sit around chatting over afternoon tea. But animals do make a variety of sounds, each of which seems to convey a different, specific meaning. The blue-nose dolphin makes at least eighteen discernible sounds, one of which is a call for help. And it works. Two dolphins will rush to the side of one which has given the distress call, hoist him to the surface of the water and stay there with him until he is able to fend for himself once more.

At the beginnings of their lives, young animals have many things to learn from their fathers and mothers, just as human babies do. Even though they don't go to school, young animals must learn how to find food, how to sense danger, how to fight—or run—for their lives.

Animals learn part of what they must know through play. Cats—from the most ferocious tigers to the gentlest house pets—start learning to stalk when they are kittens. They creep into the long grass, flatten out behind a piece of shrubbery, and wait for a careless brother or sister to pass.

12

When the unwary kitten comes by—noisily, for walking in catlike silence is something that must be learned, too—the waiting one pounces out of ambush and falls on his prey.

Over and over they roll, trying to rake one another with their rear claws, as they have seen their mother do. Then they separate, and the game, in which they learn hunting technique, begins all over again.

The cleverer an animal breed, the more there is for the animal to learn. And, although animals know some things by instinct, many of them have to be taught the skills they need to survive. Young deer are clumsy leapers; baby giraffes don't know what to do with their long legs—they must learn. And seals, walrus, otters, hippopotamuses, which spend more time in water than on land, must be taught to swim.

Animals have a variety of sleeping habits. Some need almost no sleep at all, some sleep only at night, others only during the day. And some, of course, sleep all winter long. Like people, some animals enjoy an afternoon nap and, also like people, they may have a hard time keeping the youngsters quiet while they rest. The sea otter is one of these. He likes to stretch out for a midday nap—on a comfortable bed of seaweed—but just as he drops off, along come the young otters. They pounce on top of him, duck him, poke him in the stomach. He looks like a grouchy grandfather as he retreats to another bed, hoping for a little peace and quiet this time.

The Animal Kingdom covers the whole world, and its subjects, from the tiniest shrew to the biggest elephant, can be endlessly fascinating.

13

CHAPTER

1

Dinner Time

Some diners out, such as aardvarks, prefer white ants. Others, like polar bears, think blubber a tasty delicacy

Most of an animal's waking hours are spent tracking down breakfast or smelling out dinner. If the food supply gives out in the area where an animal lives, it must move somewhere else or die of starvation. Food is life.

Some animals will eat anything they can find. Opossums are quite unparticular. Leaves, fruit, insects, small animals, dead and rotting flesh, vegetables, bread—the opossum will eat all these and anything else at hand, including other opossums.

Bears, except polar bears, are also easy to please. They like berries, grass, roots, insects, eggs, nuts, snakes, fruit. They fish for salmon, catching them in running streams with their paws. They eat any small animals, such as mice, rats and gophers, which they happen to encounter. They dig up ground squirrels and overturn rocks looking for ants.

The black bear loves honey. Since he is an excellent climber and since his thick hide gives him protection against bee stings, he is well equipped to find and take honey. While he is at it, he eats the bees, too.

At national parks, where tourists feed them, black bears dine on almost everything that humans eat, including ice cream, oranges, peanut-butter sandwiches and hot dogs.

The largest bat in the world, the flying fox, is a fruit lover. He eats hanging upside down.

The raccoon is another which is fond of the foods that humans eat. He is an inveterate night raider of garbage cans, often waking his human neighbors in the small hours as he takes off a cover, slams it down with a resounding clatter, and starts to forage.

A clever scrounger

The raccoon can be very clever about his scrounging. One observer of the Animal Kingdom, determined that there would be no more raids on his garbage, bent the lid so that it would take more than raccoon strength to remove it. That night, the raccoon simply turned the can over on its side, dragged it to the top of a hill, and gave a push. Down went the can, clattering and thumping. On its trip, the cover was knocked off. The raccoon ambled down the hill to the now-open can and proceeded to have a leisurely dinner. Garbage-can tidbits favored by the raccoon include melon rinds, tomato scraps and corn cobs to which a few succulent kernels still cling.

Some animals can eat only one particular kind of food. Vampire bats of Central and South America consume only blood from living victims. Koalas of Australia live exclusively on the leaves of eucalyptus trees.

Most animals eat whatever they can get. As eaters, they fall into two main groups. Those that live primarily on meat, fish and insects are called "carnivores"—flesh eaters. Those that live pri-

16

Bears like sweets, raid bees' nests for honey—and a tasty snack of bees, as well.

The gibbon swings through the trees by his arms with his lunch safely tucked in his feet.

marily on vegetable matter are called "herbivores"—plant eaters. But carnivores will sometimes eat grass or leaves, and herbivores will occasionally sample flesh if they are hungry enough.

Vegetable matter is much harder to digest than meat, fish or insect food. Consequently, herbivores have longer and more complicated digestive systems than do flesh eaters. When a tadpole, which eats only plants, changes into a frog, which eats only insects, his intestine shortens to about two-thirds of its previous length.

Some herbivores, such as cows, deer and antelope, may have as many as four

compartments to their stomachs for handling digestion. The animal tears off bits of grass or leaves and swallows them almost whole. The food is stored in a kind of side-pocket compartment of the animal's stomach, until he has eaten his fill. It is then brought back to the mouth, where it gets thoroughly chewed, before it is finally swallowed and digested.

Many such animals are grazers (eaters of grass), feeding on the great prairies and savannahs of the world. Most members of the ox family—antelope, pronghorns and many others—are grazers. Others are browsers (eaters of

17

No trouble feeding for the long-legged giraffe—but stooping to drink is another matter.

twigs, leaves, bark and buds), among them most members of the deer family, the giraffe and his cousin the okapi.

The black rhino has a very agile, overhanging upper lip, which he uses for plucking his food.

Very big, very deft

Elephants eat both grass and leaves. For all his size, the elephant is a very deft animal. His long, sturdy trunk can reach down to clumps of grass on the ground or up high to pluck a single small leaf. If his trunk can't reach a particular branch the elephant wants, he may just put his head against the tree and topple the whole thing over.

A small and most industrious grass eater is the pika, a cousin of the rabbit. Pikas go "haying" just like men, cutting fresh grass, bringing it to their cave homes, and spreading it out to dry. When rain threatens, they gather it all up and carry it inside. When the weather clears, the pikas spread the hay out in the sun again to continue drying.

Monkeys feed chiefly on leaves, berries and fruit. The great apes—chimpanzee, orangutan and gorilla—live almost entirely on a diet of fruit and leaves. The man-eating gorilla of the horror movies is a fairy tale—gorillas are strict vegetarians. A lesser ape, the gibbon, often swings through the trees carrying his food in his feet.

A variety of other animals feed on leaves and fruits. The flying fox is a fruit-eating bat, which does its eating while hanging upside down. Fruit-eating bats have a curious eating problem: Since they feed (as they do everything else) upside down, the juices from the fruit might run into their noses, block their breathing passages, and drown them. To prevent this, nature has supplied them with various air-storage bladders or drainage tubes, which often make their faces look distorted.

The sloths of Central America spend all their lives in trees and feed on them. The three-toed sloth eats only the flowers and leaves of the wild pawpaw.

The North American porcupine finds himself a place in a tree, starts eating the bark and leaves, and usually does not move until he has devoured everything within reach. Sometimes he doesn't come down for days.

Food for the cold winter

Another browser is the industrious beaver; he lives on bark, twigs and leaves. To make sure he has fresh food for the cold months, he anchors branches and twigs in the muddy bottom of the stream near his lodge. A hard-working beaver needn't stick his nose above water all winter long.

Hares are mostly prairie or open-field dwellers. They eat some grass and much ground leafage. Rabbits are mainly forest dwellers and live by browsing. But both will raid vegetable gardens if they have a chance.

Many animals of the Far North, such as caribou, reindeer and lemming, live

19

The gray squirrel will work very hard at gathering nuts—but really prefers to beg.

nonchalantly on the most prickly of cactus, climbing up and down by the sharp spines as if they were a ladder.

The watery parts of the world have their browsers and grazers, too. The tapir, an odd-looking creature which lives in swamps or in jungles near streams, spends most of his time in or near water and feeds on juicy reeds. Moose enjoy water plants so much that they will dive down over their heads to pluck them. Moose are great swimmers and will feed in quite deep water. If food runs low in one area, a herd of moose may swim a large lake or even an arm of the sea to reach a more promising range.

Short-time shelters

The muskrat is one of the commonest animals of the American marshes. He dines on reeds and water grasses. During bad weather, he often builds himself small, temporary feeding shelters of sticks and grass stems. There he can nibble in peace, protected from the cold.

The muskrat often builds a permanent house out of his favorite food. He first gathers reeds and water grasses and piles them up in the water until he has a high, shaggy pile. Next, he chews out a hole in the middle of the part above the water. Finally entering, he begins to eat from the inside out. The muskrat can spend the whole winter like this, dining on the inside of his house.

An animal's usual diet is related to his tooth equipment. Browsers and

on nothing but the lichen and moss that grow on the icy plains. Rocky Mountain goats and other animals which live above the tree line feed on a similar sparse diet.

Camels, gazelles and many smaller creatures which live in desert regions feed on the thorny bushes and cactus-like scrub that grow in such hot, dry lands. Many of these prickly-looking plants act as natural water-storage tanks, soaking up and retaining whatever moisture there is. A thirsty animal can obtain liquid by eating parts of these plants. Desert-dwelling mice gnaw grazers need heavy molars (grinding teeth) to break up the tough fibers of bark or pasture grass. In areas where the vegetation is particularly harsh, animals sometimes wear their teeth away completely.

Seed, nut and root eaters need sharp incisors (gnawing teeth in the front of the mouth). Among animals, these incisors are exceedingly sharp and often continue to grow throughout the animal's life. He must do a great deal of gnawing to keep them worn down, so that they will not keep on growing right

out of his mouth—then he would starve.

One of the world's great gnawers is the pocket gopher of the North American prairies. He specializes in roots—any kind of root, from a tiny peanut to the taproot of a full-grown tree. His upper front teeth, two razor-sharp chisels, are actually *outside* his mouth, protruding through an opening in the skin of his upper lip. With these teeth, he can chop out a portion of root and whittle it down to carrying size within seconds.

Like many other small animals, the

To a moose, nothing is sweeter than water plants. He will dive headfirst to get at them.

To gather up his favorite food, termites, the anteater shoots out a long, sticky tongue.

pocket gopher stores up food for the future. He is equipped with "pockets"—fur-lined pouches—in his cheeks which he fills up with pieces of root. When he has a full load, he returns to his burrow and squeezes out his cheeks with his paws, like a man squeezing a tube of toothpaste.

The pocket mouse, a tiny creature which weighs only one-third of an ounce, packs a half teaspoonful of seeds into his little cheeks. A chipmunk 4 inches long can carry up to thirty kernels of corn at one time. The little hamster, encountering an enemy during one of his foraging expeditions, simply blows his cheekful of seeds in the other's face.

To Americans, the most familiar hoarder is the Eastern gray squirrel, so common in city parks and suburban streets. He earns most of his living begging. When given a nut, he first turns it around and around with his paws, testing the soundness of the shell with his teeth. If it is cracked, he eats it then and there; if whole, he carries it off and buries it for use at some future time.

His cousin, the red squirrel of the evergreen forests, lives on the seeds of pine and spruce trees. He collects the cones, which hold the seeds, and stores them up in moist places. He also likes mushrooms. He carries them up to high, sunlit branches, where he spreads them out to dry before adding them to his hoard. With man, he shares a taste for maple syrup. He "taps" the maple tree (opens a vein to let the sap run out) by biting into the delicate bark of an upper limb and sucking the juice.

Often enough, the little hoarders of the Animal Kingdom forget where they left their buried treasure, and the seeds and nuts sprout and grow into new plants. In this way, these small creatures unwittingly become animal farmers and animal foresters.

The herbivores feed on the plant world. The carnivores feed on the herbivores. In habits of life, in physical make-up, the two kinds of animals are very different.

The teeth of the carnivore are adapted for chopping and biting. His incisors are tiny, and his molars have jagged edges instead of being flat on top. As a rule, his jaws can only be moved up and down instead of from side to side like a cow's or a man's. So, since he cannot chew his food, he tears it off and gulps it down almost whole.

The carnivore eats only now and then,

but it is a big meal. One feast may last him for two days or more. Snakes may go as long as six months on one meal.

The carnivore is equipped to be a hunter. His eyes are on the front of his head, because he must be able to see in depth and gauge distance with accuracy. The carnivore usually has claws of some kind on all four feet, for scratching his prey or for digging into the ground for a firm stance.

Being a successful hunter in the Animal Kingdom requires skill and practice. Every carnivore has his own technique.

A foe to be reckoned with

When seen above ground, the mole looks like a helpless wretch—too blind to see his enemies, too round to run from them, too small to fight back. But in his own world, which lies below the surface of the ground, he is a foe to be reckoned with.

Using his spade-like front teeth and powerful paws to claw out the dirt, he tunnels away at 2½ miles per hour—the speed of a man's slow walk. His hearing is extremely sharp. His snout and tail are both very sensitive feelers. Nothing edible escapes him. He eats his weight in insects every day, taking a full meal every six or seven hours. He starves to death if deprived of food for more than half a day. More tasty to him than insects, however, are earthworms. Encountering one, he pins it down. Then he smooths it out with his paws, flicks away the dirt, and finishes it.

23

Flattening himself on the ice, the polar bear stalks dinner that is both fast and wary. Arctic

Many animals take insects as part of their diet, but certain creatures make such a specialty of insect-eating that their bodies are literally built with that kind of food—and that sort of specialized digestive system—in mind.

The giant anteater of the Central and South American jungle stands 2 feet high and 3 or 4 feet long—plus 4 more feet of plume-like tail. Its head looks like a frying-pan handle; the mouth at the front end is a tiny hole. On his front feet are three huge claws. He is amazingly strong for his size.

He needs these advantages, for the nests of termites—his favorite food—are rock-hard fortresses. The anteater attacks with determination and sharp claws and rips out a hole in the wall or collapses part of the roof of the nest. When the insects come swarming out, he extends his long, sticky tongue and rakes in his dinner of termites.

If it were not for specialists like the anteater, the fast-breeding tropical insects might soon swarm out of control.

The mink and the otter are fish lovers. Both live near streams. Both catch fish, frogs and small animals that live in water. The badger and the polecat are bigger members of the weasel family. They live in underground burrows and

cold makes game scarce, so the bear must be certain to judge his distance right the first try.

dig out ground squirrels and pocket gophers for food.

Pound for pound, members of the weasel family are possibly the most fearsome animals on land. The largest of them, the wolverine, is no bigger than a stocky water spaniel, but he can pull down a caribou.

Another creature very justly feared for his cunning and his hunting skill is the great white polar bear. Like most bears, he will eat vegetable matter when it is available, but this is rare in the Far North, and consequently, the polar bear eats small creatures like lemmings, seabirds and fish.

His favorite food is seals. Sometimes he lies in wait by the telltale opening that marks the air hole of a ringed seal. He knows the seal must come up to breathe every few minutes. At other times he may find a herd of seals resting on the ice. This is good luck. Where there are no mounds to hide behind, the polar bear flattens himself against the ice and approaches at a creep, his yellow-white coat blending with the Arctic landscape. When he is close enough for the kill, he does it with one blow from his mighty paw.

All members of the cat family are carnivores and all are gifted hunters.

25

Most of them, like the tiger of Asia and the leopard of Africa, are forest animals and hunt alone, relying on stealth. Most savage and unpredictable of the great cats is probably the leopard. He watches troups of baboons, waiting for a straggler. He follows herds of antelope, looking for a chance to cut one out. He marks the favorite haunts of his victims and lies in ambush. He will not attack man unless provoked, but he raids farms and villages.

When he has eaten his fill, he leaves the rest of the carcass hanging in a tree, where jackals cannot get at it. Some-times these leopard larders are branches 20 feet off the ground.

The jaguar, the great spotted cat of Central America, is probably the most versatile of the cat hunters. He can swim. He can climb trees. He is at home in the mountains, in the jungle, in the marshes. He catches fish. He overturns turtles and rips them from their shells. He kills deer, cattle and wild pigs. He can break the neck of a full-grown ox. Unlike tigers, lions, leopards, pumas and all other great cats, the jaguar *will* attack man deliberately.

One of the most remarkable cat hunt-

The jaguar, a clever hunter, usually catches whatever he is pursuing—even the deadly boa.

The caracal, a champion jumper, leaps high into the air to catch his dinner of birds.

ers is the cheetah. He lives on the plains and in desert regions, rather than the forest. He hunts by swiftly overtaking his victims, rather than by slowly creeping up on them. He is believed to be the fastest runner in the Animal Kingdom.

The specialty of the caracal is leaping—he can jump 5 or 6 feet off the ground from a standing start. In India, he is trained for bird hunting. He is so fast that when let loose amid a flock of pigeons, he can kill a full dozen before the birds have time to take alarm and scatter. In the wild, he occasionally runs down the swift gazelle.

Most seals and whales live in "pods" (herds) and hunt in pods, following schools of fish or octopuses or krill (minute shellfish). The more plentiful the food, the larger the herd of sea animals gathered together. A herd of walrus, having found a good clam bed, settles down and feeds until the supply runs low.

Lions are not greedy or bloodthirsty creatures. One kill may last a pair for a full week, and while they have meat available, they do not hunt. The heavy work of finding dinner is done by the lioness. She picks out a good place for an ambush—beside a water hole, perhaps, or near her victim's favorite grazing land. Her mate takes his position upwind, so that their prey can catch smell of him. The lions are after big game—waterbuck, wildebeest, giraffe, or their favorite, zebra. Their victim, scenting an enemy, moves away from the lion and toward his mate, while she creeps closer and closer until she is within 100 yards. Then she closes in.

The lioness kills like a bear, with one swipe of her paw.

The killer whale *is* greedy and bloodthirsty. Moreover, he is large—20 to 30 feet in length—the swiftest swimmer in the seas and full of cunning. He hunts in a pack of forty or more.

Deep-sea teamwork

Killer whales have many tactics. Sighting a school of small white whales or seals, they may separate, each big killer pouncing on his own victim. Or, faced with a larger foe, like the gray whale, the entire pack may circle it, each one snatching a mouthful. They will leave the water in chase of prey if they have to, lunging out on an ice shelf to snap at huskies or lounging seals. Sometimes they ram the ice from below, the pack working in unison, in an effort to break it and topple the seals into the water.

The real expert at pack hunting is the Cape hunting dog of Africa. His hunting technique is simple: run his prospective dinner off its legs. A pack may have as many as sixty members. When the antelope start to move, the race is on. Sooner or later the dogs catch up. The antelope may slash back with sharp horns and hoofs—he may wound or kill a dog or two. But there are dozens more. Sooner or later he falls, exhausted.

The wolf is the largest and strongest of the dog family—and, in many ways,

the cleverest, too. The wolf pack is a family group. There may be three to six adult animals—father, mother, two or three of their young from previous years' litters—plus a new litter of young puppies. They hunt for dinner of caribou, moose, sometimes even bison—all animals weighing many times what a wolf weighs. To succeed, they need close cooperation and many tricks.

Wolves may send a scout or two up ahead to sniff out a herd of caribou or moose and signal the others with barks or howls. Having caught up with the herd, they may content themselves with prowling the outskirts, snatching off an

Few animals can outrun the quick, relentless Cape hunting dogs once the pack is on the chase

unwary calf. But if the caribou are alert, and there aren't many sick or young animals, the hunting is harder.

Caribou are much faster than wolves, but the wolf has endurance. He can keep up a steady pace of 20 miles per hour all night long. When a caribou begins to tire, the wolves close in—snarling and leaping, tearing at its flanks, nipping them and dodging away.

Sometimes, particularly in autumn when he has his full rack of antlers, a bull caribou may choose to stand and fight. He can be a deadly enemy, but the wolves do not hesitate. Two or three keep him busy—one gashing at his hind legs while another leaps at the throat, nimbly dodging the swift sharp antlers. Meanwhile, the rest of the pack circles to raid unprotected females and calves.

Some carnivores do little or no hunting of their own, but depend on leftovers and scraps from the hunts of others. The jackal hangs about near a group of feeding lions and waits his chance to sneak in and finish off the carcass. Hyenas are free-lance carrion eaters, scouting for anything dead.

These eaters of carrion are among the most useful of animals. Without them, the woods and forests and deserts would become vast, smelly garbage pails.

These animals hunt in the high, open country of Africa. They can outrun even the swift gazelle.

CHAPTER

2

Bedtime

Some sleepers make their beds high in treetops. Others pick the ocean as the perfect place for a comfortable snooze

An animal's bed may be the branch of a tree, a hole in the ground, even an ocean swell. Some animals are happy to drop down anywhere. Others are more particular where they sleep.

The great apes make new sleeping quarters almost every night. The chimpanzee makes a kind of mattress by bending tree branches together and then weaving in smaller branches. For more comfort, he covers the branches with twigs and leaves.

A chimp usually has a second bed on the ground for daytime naps. This is built crudely of leaves and branches, but it gives the chimpanzee shade from the hot tropical sun while he snoozes.

The orangutan and the gorilla are nest builders. The female gorilla builds her nest in the trees and sleeps there with her babies. The male gorilla weighs too much to be a tree sleeper. He piles up a soft bed on the ground, at the foot of the tree, and keeps guard.

One ape that really likes his sleep is the orangutan. He may work an hour or more making his bed, weaving the nest with loving care, testing the branches to make sure they will hold his great weight. He leaves part of one branch sticking out, and this becomes his "handle" branch; he uses it to haul himself into and out of his nest. When he finally

The mother sloth's body, hanging upside down from a branch, makes a safe cradle for her baby.

has his bed ready, he crawls inside, pulls more leaves over him like a blanket and snuggles down.

The great apes are the only animals that make beds—that is, places used only for sleeping. Other tree dwellers simply cling to the nearest comfortable bough. They can do this because they are specially equipped for keeping these precarious perches while sleeping.

Monkeys, for instance, have special reflexes for holding on. Human hands, if relaxed, will fall half open. When a monkey's hands—and feet—are relaxed, they clench like fists. An African monkey may sleep in treetops 100 feet from the ground, his fingers snapped tight around the nearest handhold.

Stranger still is the way the potto, a distant cousin of the monkey, sleeps. He

The orangutan makes his bed in a tree. A branch, sticking out, serves as a handle.

Clutching a stalk of bamboo with clasped fingers, the tarsier sleeps comfortably.

has feet that work like suction cups. The palms are heavily padded, while the big toes are extra long. Once he clamps his padded feet around a tree limb, he is fastened tight. Even if he dies while asleep, his feet will not let go.

The tarsier is a tiny creature, all eyes and great long fingers. He likes to leap about at night and sleep during the day. He sleeps upright, his bed a stalk of bamboo or dangling vine. Clasping the stalk with his fingers, like a man holding a golf club, he puts his tail down the vine as a brace.

Whales, dolphins and some seals feel there is nothing so comfortable as a nice, soft stretch of water for sleeping.

The bottle-nose dolphin floats just below the surface, closing and opening his eyes every fifteen to thirty seconds. A gentle stroke with his tail brings him to the surface for a breath of air.

Atlantic gray seals sleep in this same manner, rising and sinking between breaths. Often they remain underwater five minutes or longer at a time.

Actually, sea mammals need less rest than land animals. They do not need to use energy holding themselves up or running or climbing. Their bodies are supported by the pressure of the water. In a way, whales and dolphins may be said to spend the whole day in bed.

A seagoing cradle

The sea otter also sleeps in water, provided the sea is smooth (in rough weather he goes ashore). He sleeps at the surface, usually in a bed of seaweed, which keeps him from drifting. He lies on his back, face out of the water. His forepaws cover his eyes or rest on his chest, while his hind flippers make light swishes in the lapping waves. If a female otter has a baby to take care of, she puts him to sleep on her chest, turning herself into a seagoing cradle.

The walrus and many seals choose sleeping quarters that seem uninviting to humans—rocky beaches or ice floes.

The walrus is fond of sleep and exceedingly cross when his slumber is interrupted. He lives in a herd, which at times numbers thousands of animals, and sleeps packed in tightly with his neighbors. Often tusks and whiskers get in the way, or one walrus accidently pokes his neighbor. The prodded walrus rears up with a roar and jabs about him

The sea otter sleeps on his back in the water, his paws comfortable on his chest.

with his tusks. Sometimes he catches the real offender, sometimes an innocent bystander. His victims, of course, rise up and jab others, until soon the entire herd is in an uproar.

The raccoon is on the move at night and sleeps during the day. Like the cat, he enjoys the warm feel of the sun on his fur. Often he will find a sunny tree limb and stretch out on his back, with his forepaws over his eyes.

Some very strange beds

The noolbenger, a small pouched animal of Australia, sleeps in old birds' nests, sitting upright. The koala finds a tree crotch into which he can wedge himself; then he folds his four limbs over his stomach and clutches his hind paws with his hands.

Some animals make special arrangements for comfort. Normally, the jackal digs a hole in the ground to sleep in. But when the weather is hot, he may do his sleeping in shallow water.

Animals with bushy tails often put them to good use for sleeping comfort. The tree squirrel sometimes uses his tail as a pillow and often uses it as a blanket, wrapping it around himself in the cold weather. Since he sleeps outdoors—on the ground—even in the coldest weather, the red fox has even greater need for his thick tail. He curls up in a circle, nose resting on toes, and covers himself with his warm brush.

Most animals lie down to sleep or curl up in some fashion. But not all. For some creatures, it is more comfortable to stand up. When the horse lies down, his great weight presses on his lungs, making it hard for him to breathe. He prefers to spend most of the night standing. He has special locking muscles in his legs. As he relaxes and falls asleep, his knees lock in place. That way, he is firmly braced and will not fall down.

The elephant of Africa, the largest of living land animals, is another that often sleeps standing up. He takes his rest in two shifts, a nap in the middle of the day and a somewhat longer rest in the middle of the night. Sometimes he props his massive tusks in a convenient tree crotch. His Asiatic cousin, which is somewhat smaller and has smaller tusks, is more likely to lie down to sleep, but even he often sleeps on his feet during his midday nap or when he is feeling ill. Both African and Asiatic elephants snore loudly through their trunks.

The hippopotamus is another stander. He is a heavy animal, but he spends most of his time in water, which provides support for his bulk. The hippopotamus is nocturnal and does his sleeping during the day—usually in a patch of reeds along the bank of a river. Sometimes he rests his massive head on his neighbor's back; sometimes he sinks so deep that only his round nostrils and bony eye sockets are visible.

The rhinoceros is another large and heavy animal, but his size doesn't seem

The koala sleeps wedged into the crotch of a tree, clutching his feet with both his hands.

The hippopotamus, a nocturnal animal, does all his heavy sleeping during the day and most of his

to make much difference to his sleeping posture. Like chimpanzees, sea otters and elephants, he likes to take an extra nap in the middle of the day. He picks a shady spot and then may either stand up or lie down; if he lies down, he may either stretch out or tuck his feet under him like a cat.

Birds often take up sleeping positions that seem strange to humans. The ptarmigan and the snow bunting keep warm by burrowing under the snow to sleep, while the sophisticated city starling roosts near electric signs—they keep

his feet warm on the coldest days.

An animal may sleep lightly or deeply, often or seldom. He may change his sleeping habits with the season of the year or the time of day. His body may demand more or less sleep than the bodies of other animals. Then, again, some animals simply like to sleep more than other animals do.

Cud-chewing animals, like cows, sheep, goats, camels, llamas, deer and antelope, seem to be short, light sleepers.

Lions will lie at their ease near their half-eaten meal and sleep "with one eye

feeding at night. When he snoozes, another hippo's broad flank makes a nice, comfortable pillow.

open" to make sure that no jackal or vulture steals their property. The tiger does the same, often remaining for days, alternately eating and sleeping.

Snakes are also light sleepers, scientists believe. A snake has no eyelids and cannot close his eyes, so it cannot be determined that he actually does sleep. However, he often remains quiet and unmoving for long spells, and it is thought that these rest periods are the snake's way of sleeping. If so, he is indeed a light sleeper! For he cannot hear at all, and yet the smallest disturbance sends him up and away in a flash.

The giraffe alternates between deep and light sleep. For four or five minutes at a time he sleeps soundly, lying down, head resting on his own flank. Then he stretches his long neck out on the ground—or rises and holds it erect, knees locking—and finishes up with a light doze.

The heavy sleepers, by and large, are those animals that are well armed against their enemies. The badger with his thick skin is a heavy sleeper; so are the prickly hedgehog and porcupine, the

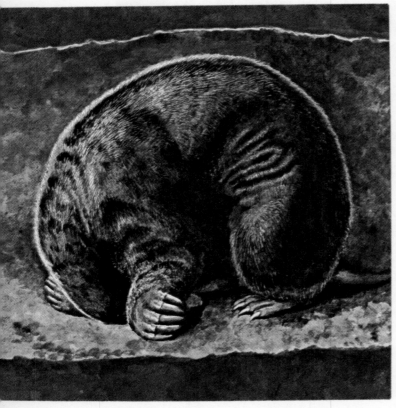

The European mole, a heavy sleeper, tucks his head snugly in between his front legs.

can be picked up without his waking up.

Some flying creatures, like bats, hummingbirds and chimney swifts, are such deep sleepers that they actually enter short states resembling hibernation. Their body temperatures fall 10 or 15 degrees, their heartbeats slow down, and their bodies' functions go into slow motion.

Living at a breakneck pace

Probably the most sleepless of all mammals are the many varieties of shrews. This tiny, insect-eating creature lives at a breakneck pace. To stay alive, he must have more than his full body weight in food every day, so he eats constantly. With his routine of eating, catching more food, and eating again, the shrew has little time for sleep.

At the other end of the scale is the sluggish sloth of Central America. He is easily the most talented sleeper in the Animal Kingdom—eighteen hours a day is his minimum. And even when he is awake, he is not apt to bestir himself greatly.

The sloth is well equipped for the lazy life. His long fur and thick skin protect him against all but the largest of enemies. His curved claws—like immense hooks on all four feet—enable him to live almost entirely in the trees, where larger animals cannot get at him. He spends most of his life hanging upside down. He hooks his claws over a tree limb, preferably a drooping branch so that his front quarters hang lower

beaver in his well-protected house, the little skunk with his long-distance weapon.

Burrowing mammals, which have snug and well-hidden dens underground, can also afford to sleep long and deeply. The woodchuck does not emerge from his hole until the day is well advanced.

Sleepier yet is the European mole. He puts his head down between his front legs and rests part of his weight on it. Then, sitting half on his head, he goes off into a deep sleep. So deep, in fact, that his den can be broken open and he

The chipmunk works hard to gather stores for the cold weather. Then he retires for long winter sleep curled on top of his pile of nuts and seeds, which serves as bed and snack bar as well.

than his hind quarters. There he stays—whether asleep or awake.

Some animals spend months at a time in a state of deep sleep—so deep that their bodies' functions are slowed down almost to stopping. This state is called *hibernation* when it takes place in the winter, or *estivation* when it takes place in summer.

The chipmunk is one hibernator. He sleeps alone, accompanied only by a huge pile of nuts and seeds. He goes to sleep lying on top of his supplies, and when he wakes up during the winter, he eats. By springtime, he has usually eaten his way down to the bottom. The woodchuck, on the other hand, likes company during his winter sleep. Two, four, or even six woodchucks may hibernate in the same den.

Animals hibernate in order to survive the cold and estivate in order to survive a dry season. As a rule, an animal does either one or the other, but some do both. The American ground squirrel, for instance, remains asleep for up to eight months of the year.

A hibernating animal is usually one

which has a home-place den or nest. (Bats are one exception.) He spends the summer either building a new one or enlarging and improving the old. In autumn, when insects are plentiful and the trees are covered with seeds and fruits, he eats and eats and eats, building up fat. As the season grows colder, it becomes time to go to sleep. He retires to his den, closes off the entrance, and settles down.

In hibernation, the animal's temperature goes down far below normal. The woodchuck's normal temperature is 100 degrees, but when he hibernates, it may drop to half that or even lower. Bats, with a normal temperature of 104 de-

grees, have been found hibernating at 40 to 50 degrees.

In hibernation, the heartbeat and breathing of the animal slow down. From 300 beats a minute, his heart may slow to 10 beats or so. From 70 breaths per minute, his breathing may slow to an average of 4 or 5. Many of his organs stop working. He is unconscious.

It usually takes several days for an animal to fall into a sleep this deep. Once in it, he rouses from time to time during the winter, stirring and warming up. If there is food stored in his burrow, he may nibble on it. Bats drink lots of water. Some animals go outside for a stroll. But after a brief recess, the hi-

Female bears retire to shelter for their long winter sleep. But male bears curl up in a convenient hollow on the bare ground, with the fallen snow to serve as a cozy blanket.

The badger often wakens from his winter sleep to go outside in search of a snack.

bernating animal returns to his bedroom and drops back into his deep sleep.

Many kinds of hedgehogs and mice are hibernators. In dry climates, hedgehogs also estivate. For summer use, they build nests near or on the surface of the ground. But for winter, they find deeper, warmer quarters, usually holes in soft hillsides or under fallen logs. They line these with grass and leaves.

Many reptiles, amphibians and fish hibernate, too. Most snakes, with their soft noses and legless bodies, are unable to dig burrows of their own, so they often use the abandoned shelters of other animals.

Some freshwater fish enter a kind of hibernation, remaining still and unmoving at the bottom of ponds and lakes.

Many animals which are not true hibernators nevertheless spend the winter mostly in sleep. The bear, the badger and the raccoon are a few. Their temperature goes down a few degrees, and they become muddleheaded and slow.

The female bear usually spends the winter in a cave—that is where she gives birth, and the cubs need shelter. But the happy-go-lucky male is perfectly content with a sheltered hollow or a leaf-filled depression in the ground. Often, his fur becomes iced over or covered with snow while he sleeps.

The badger makes regular excursions from his burrow, trundling across the snow in search of food. The raccoon, too, frequently leaves his tree hole and climbs down and hunts for a snack.

Time to get up

When spring comes, the hibernating animal slowly warms up, shakes off his winter grogginess and emerges from his burrow. He is thin, having lived mainly off his stored-up fat all winter long. But he does have a reserve left. This reserve is called "recovery fat," and it tides him over until, in the warming days of spring, he feeds, gains back strength and becomes his old self again.

Much less is known about estivation than about hibernation. However, scientists believe that the two states are very much alike. When streams begin to dry up, the estivating animal burrows into the mud or clay at the water's edge. The mud keeps him damp and shields him from the sun. In this condition, he sleeps until he can safely emerge.

41

Home Sweet Home

Home can be a cozy cave, a tunnel with several rooms, a perch high up in a tree, or just a smooth stalk of bamboo

Where does an animal live? Why, at his home—shelter of some kind suited to his needs.

If he is a long-legged animal, a swift runner, he may need only to stand under a tree occasionally. If he is weak and slow, he may need a very strong and well-hidden house for protection. If he lives near water, he may make his home in the bank of a river. If he is a mountain animal, he may take shelter behind crags and pinnacles of rock. Some animals take shelter every day. Others need it only in bad weather or during the breeding season when there are young to be protected.

There are two main kinds of animal homes, holes and nests. The perfect hole is a cave—sturdy, well insulated against cold or heat and ready-made. A hole-living animal will almost always take a cave if he finds one and is allowed to remain unmolested. A single large cave may offer shelter to a dozen different kinds of animals—snakes, rats and mice, lizards, fish, coyotes, insects, birds. And crannies between large rocks make little, one-room caves for smaller creatures.

Wolves often have their headquarters in caves. Living as they do in Alaska, Siberia and other sub-Arctic lands, they need staunch protection against bitter cold. Wolves are roamers by necessity,

Wood rats, always on the hunt for building materials, sometimes rob campers of buttons, coins.

following routes possibly 100 miles in circumference in pursuit of their food. But they are also family animals, mating for life and remaining together in family groups. A cave provides a safe place in which to leave the cubs and sick or wounded adults while the others are on the hunt.

Cave dwellers tend to be medium-size—small enough to need a safe hideaway, but large enough to take over a cave and keep other animals out. In the cat family, the very powerful members —tigers, lions, leopards, jaguars—have no fixed place to live, but find temporary shelters in which to eat or sleep.

The little members—bobcats, African wildcats, ocelots, margays—often take shelter in trees. But the caracal—the golden cat of Africa—the puma, the cheetah and the sand cat of Arabia are cave animals.

Some bears are cave dwellers—chiefly female bears, usually in wintertime. Too big to be attacked, too well-furred to need much shelter, bears like to roam. But the cubs are born in winter, and for their safety the mother must see that she has a well-protected spot in which to pass the cold months. Polar-bear mothers in the Arctic excavate burrows in the snow, which are then warmed by

When hunting is good, the wolf—a family man—works hard to store up a surplus of food.

The raccoon, a good climber, makes himself a safe and comfortable home in a tree hole.

the animals' own body temperature—as are the igloos of Eskimos.

Natural rock piles—formed by avalanches or by the breaking up of great rock faces—offer many small caves. Great colonies of whistling pikas, the rock hyraxes of Africa and the mountain chinchillas of South America make their homes in rock piles.

The pika likes to sit out on the warm rock face during the heat of the day and take a good sunbath, keeping up a shrill whistling.

Another kind of natural hole is a hollow in a tree. For most animals, tree holes are like caves—found, not made. And, like caves, tree holes are highly thought of as homes, being safe, comfortable, dry and cozy.

Porcupines, bobcats, raccoons, squirrels, crested hamsters of East Africa, all live in tree holes for at least a part of the year.

Most animals that live in tree holes bring nesting materials to make a soft lining for their ready-made houses. The phascogale, a pouched rat of Australia, steals paper for this purpose, sometimes even bank notes. Flying phalangers, pouched creatures like flying squirrels, are exceedingly fussy about the linings of their nests. One species will travel a quarter of a mile to find exactly what he is looking for. All of them carry home the bundles of materials for their nests in their curled-up tails.

Sinking like a swamped boat

There are many talented hole diggers in the Animal Kingdom. Wombats dig tunnels 15 to 100 feet long, ending in large and luxurious nesting chambers. The eleven-banded armadillo digs shafts as much as 50 feet deep, straight down. When digging in a hurry, the aardvark can send a jet of earth 2 feet thick shooting 12 feet into the air. The spiny anteater digs with all four feet; instead of diving underground headfirst, he simply sinks like a swamped boat.

Moles and gophers live underground almost entirely, emerging only at rare intervals, and dig tunnels as their way of walking abroad in search of food. The pocket gopher can dig a tunnel 200 feet long in a single night. Both gophers and moles have a double set of tunnels— one for food-seeking, about 18 inches below the surface, and the other the actual dwelling place, 4 or 5 feet down. They can apparently gauge depth accurately, for their tunnels seldom rise

The aardvark is probably the fastest digger of

or sink beyond the standard depth.

Staunch diggers indeed are the badgers, surpassing even moles and gophers in speed and endurance. The badger is a great homebody and family man. He devotes much care to his burrow. Several generations of badgers may occupy the same burrow, grown-up cubs often bringing home a mate and moving in with—or next door to—the old folks.

Badgers are house proud

The European badger is a forest animal and his burrows, called "sets," are usually dug into banks or hillsides. They are much more elaborate than those of the American badger, for he is a shyer and more retiring animal. The tunnels of his set may wander about underground for 300 feet or more, and living chambers may be three stories deep.

Badgers are exceedingly house proud. The European badger is forever enlarging his set, cleaning it out, bringing in fresh bedding. Cutting piles of grass, weeds, moss or straw, he brings them back to the set entrance in his mouth. Then, when he has a large enough pile, he pulls it together into a bundle, which he holds between his nose and front paws, and backs down into the set. In spring he may cover his bed with a layer of flower petals. If the badger family is large, it takes several nights of patient labor to bring home enough fresh bedding for everyone.

The chipmunk displays his ingenuity by hiding the entrance to his hole. He first digs a sloping tunnel down to about 5 feet below ground level. There, he excavates several rooms, depending on the size of his family and the amount of nuts he has to store. Then he digs up again to the ground, making his back door. This second opening has no telltale pile of dirt, no torn-up plants to give away its position. All the dirt has been carried out through the first opening and scattered, the plants hardly disturbed. When this second entrance is ready, the first is plugged up, and the chipmunk's home is indeed hard to spot.

Coyotes make quite elaborate dens with two tunnels, each 25 or 30 feet long from the outside to the sleeping

any living creature. His great claws and his powerful leg muscles send a jet of dirt flying.

chamber below. Liking ventilation, they dig an air shaft through the roof of the chamber—or place the chamber underneath an abandoned gopher hole.

Hole dwellers often live in large communities of dozens of individuals, whose dens are connected by a maze of underground tunnels and passages. European rabbits occupy just such vast burrows, called "warrens." Fennecs, banded mongooses, certain armadillos and rat kangaroos also live in communal burrows.

Vizcachas, South American relatives of the chinchilla, live in communities of twelve to fifteen burrows, holding twice that many animals and covering an area about the size of a football field. The entrance to each den is a good 3 feet wide, and the vizcachas are careful to remove all plants, to allow a clear view. In front of these large doorways they keep piles of old bones, rocks, stolen bits of human glitter and other keepsakes, and there they sit of an evening, enjoying the air.

One of the most remarkable burrowers in the Animal Kingdom is the prairie dog. He is considered a pest by farmers and is today kept under population control, but at one time his vast "towns" covered miles of prairie land. One such community is reported to have been 25,000 miles square with a population of

The vizcacha lives in a crowded den. In front of his doorway he hoards a heap of bones.

approximately 400 million.

A prairie dog's burrow is unlike that of any other animal. It begins with a volcano-like mound, 1 or 2 feet high, on which the animal sits and looks out for enemies. The center of this mound is a hole, opening on to a vertical shaft, which drops straight down for 14 or 16 feet. There is a small alcove a foot or so from the top of this shaft, and this is used as a listening post. When alarmed, the animal ducks into this alcove, waits a moment, listening, and then peeks out. At the bottom, the tunnel turns at a right angle and becomes horizontal, widening out into the usual sleeping chambers. Finally it takes an upward turn and runs vertically for 6 to 8 feet. This second vertical shaft is used as an air lock and escape hatch.

Many animals simply live under things—under fallen logs, under shrubs, under tree roots, under stones. Often skunks, gray foxes and other bold little

48

creatures make their homes under the foundations of people's houses. The hedgehog will hole up anywhere. And there is a small South American deer, called a brocket, which makes itself arbors under trees.

A nest may be anything from a few grass stalks gathered into a protective heap to an elaborate structure housing many thousands of individual animals. It may be meant to last for a season or for a generation. It may be easy to spot or so cunningly hidden that it looks like part of the landscape.

A nest of mud and spider web

Birds' nests are not homes at all, but merely cradles for the fledglings. Nevertheless, birds' nests often are remarkable little structures, sturdy, handsome, comfortable. The Baltimore oriole and his relatives weave sack-like bags, which they suspend from tree branches. Some of these are 5 feet long. The hummingbird shapes a cup, the size of a quarter, out of mud and spider web. The ovenbird of South America builds a foot-high hump out of clay with a hollow interior and a side entrance.

Flamingos make pedestals of mud with a cup-like top. Chimney swifts construct nests of twigs and saliva which they attach to the inside of chimney walls. Their cousins, the Asiatic swifts, make nests entirely of saliva, and it is these nests that the Chinese use in their famous "bird's-nest soup."

The sociable weaverbirds of South Africa construct apartment houses and live together in communities of twenty to three hundred pairs. Under a communal roof—which is usually fastened

The tiny mouse opossum uses his handy grasping tail to transport his bedding to his nest.

49

The pretty home of the harvest mouse is a well-woven ball of grass, supported by stalks.

to a sturdy thorn tree and woven of grass—each pair builds its own little chamber.

Some birds' nests are so sturdily built that they are used over again year after year. The bald-eagle nests are gigantic masses of sticks and mud, added to every year. Some such nests weigh more than a ton. Trees often collapse under the weight of an eagle's nest.

The nests of many smaller birds are also sturdy. Frequently animals move in after the birds have left and renovate to suit themselves. White-footed mice find old birds' nests most convenient, needing only to be roofed over. The tiny mouse opossum of South and Central America does not build a roof, but lines the nest with green leaves.

A great deal of skill goes into the weaving of a harvest mouse's nest. Both American and European species live in tall grass and reeds. Both weave round nests the size of oranges, which they wedge among supporting stalks. The outside walls are of grass stems, twisted in and out by the mouse's deft fore-paws, and the inside is lined with well-chopped grass or leaves.

Under a blanket of snow

These fragile-looking little balls are surprisingly stout, well insulated against cold, wind and rain. A female mouse may occupy one all summer long, raising one litter after another. Lemmings, which build similar nests, live in them all winter, snug beneath the snow.

Most hares and rabbits make nests on the surface of the ground, usually in reeds or tall grass or under shrubbery. They are not the skilled weavers that harvest mice are. A hare's nest, called a "hide" or a "form," is usually nothing more than a bowl-shaped depression, scooped out of the ground and lined with grass or the mother's fur.

The Eastern cottontail takes great pains to hide her nest. She builds it under bushes or in dense grass. She visits it only at night, and when she departs in the morning, she covers up the babies with grass and fur and then screens that with a top layer of leaves.

"Underpasses" in the forest

Hares, rabbits, mice, moles, rats, shrews, guinea pigs and other small and helpless creatures of the woods and fields often build runways for themselves under the grass or the leaf mold on the forest floor. These "underpasses" enable them to search for food in greater safety. Half rooted out, half chewed out, they may crisscross an entire meadow and yet be unseen by other larger animals and men.

The industrious wood rat builds a permanent home and keeps adding to it and repairing it summer after summer. He first chooses a sheltered location—a low tree, a cave, an opening between rocks or cactus, a natural crevice—then begins to pile up sticks and branches until he has a high, dome-shaped mass. Inside there may be several rooms and

Beavers work in teams. If the family dam needs some shoring up, a whole crew of busy relativ

tunnels, depending on how many rats are in residence (often several families share quarters) and how long they have been at work. Large nests may stand 5 or 6 feet high and have roofs studded with cactus spikes to discourage enemies.

The wood rat is often called the "trade rat" or the "pack rat," because of his habit of carrying off small objects and leaving other things in their place. He may exchange a stone for a button, a stick for a coin. It depends on whether the new object seems to him better house-building material than the old.

When the beaver is building his house, an entire landscape may be changed. The beaver is not just a carpenter—he is an engineer. In the course of construct-

ing his lodge, he may erect a dam, dig a canal, fell trees and strip away underbrush. He may turn a brook into a pond and a forest into a swamp. He may establish a much-needed program for conserving water, or he may ruin an area that once functioned well.

He begins his chores by gnawing down a tree, perhaps 4 inches thick. This takes him fifteen minutes. (He can fell trees up to 5 feet in diameter and more than 100 feet tall, but seldom bothers.) Having eaten off the tasty bark, he cuts the tree with his sharp teeth into pieces and transports the trunk to the stream site he has chosen. He dives in, dragging the trunk, and lays it on the bottom, where he anchors

52

turns out to get the job done efficiently.

it in place with a stone. He repeats this process again and again and again, night after night, until he has raised a great mass of tree trunks across the stream, butt ends toward the current. Then he plasters this mass with mud, stones and sticks until it is a solid, watertight wall.

Soon, of course, he strips the stream banks of trees and must go farther inland to fetch them. To make his hauling job easier, he levels the ground into "logging trails" or digs canals. These canals are 6 to 18 inches deep, 2 to 30 feet wide and up to 600 feet long. If the stream has a strong current, the beaver may build a diversion dam upstream to ward off the full force of the water,

which might destroy his home dam.

Working in teams, beavers perform amazing feats of construction—dams 12 feet high, 15 to 20 feet thick, 300 feet long. One beaver dam, on the Jefferson River in Montana, measured 2,140 feet in length.

Next comes the lodge. This is a mass of sticks and rocks and mud piled up in the water itself, behind the dam. As the dammed-up water rises, so does the lodge, until it tops the dam by several feet. The entrance is below water, a narrow shaft curving upward. The living quarters, however, are above water level, dry and cozy, and often contain several rooms, a special nursery for the young and snug bedchambers. An air vent is left in the roof. A beaver deserts his dam and lodge only when the stream becomes too silted up with mud for the deep water that he needs.

All together, now

A common practice in some parts of the Animal Kingdom is for different species to live together. Rattlesnakes move in with prairie dogs, white-footed mice share a tree hole with bees, armadillos crash a rabbit's home. The yard-wide doors of the vizcacha's home provide a welcome for snakes and birds. Sometimes a guest eats his host or his host's children, but often enough they all live together in peace.

Having a suitable home can be as important to an animal as having a good meal. Both mean life to him.

53

CHAPTER

4

Togetherness

**Many animals are happiest
in a crowd. Together they "shop"
for dinner, hunt new homes,
seek nurseries for their children**

Some animals do not rely on homes to provide them with shelter and protection—they rely on one another. These are herd animals—flocks of sheep, prides of lions, troops of monkeys, all animals that live in groups and depend on their unity for survival.

Herds come in all sizes, but the basic unit usually is small—not more than a dozen or so.

A herd may be confined to the members of one family—father, mother, two or three grown children and the newly born young. Or it may be this family plus the grandparents and the cousins. It may be one male plus a group of females which he has collected into a harem for one season only. Or the herd may be an entirely female or entirely male group.

It may even be a vast collection of animals of all ages and both sexes, but if so, it is probably composed of many smaller family units. A large herd is really a group of groups.

Caribou and elk are true herd animals. Their lives follow a kind of yearly pattern, keyed to the condition of the male's antlers. The antlers begin to grow in the spring, sprouting from button-like places on the animal's head. A yearling elk produces only one little prong on each antler, but the older he

When two bull elks do battle over a herd of females, noise of the fight can be heard for miles.

gets, the more tines (branches or points) he has, until he reaches his prime. At the age of four or five, a lordly bull may sport a magnificent rack (set of antlers) 5 feet across. While they are growing, the elk spends the summer browsing in upland pastures and woods.

The antlers are full grown by September. The bull then scrapes off the velvet (soft, hairy skin that covers the growing antlers), sharpens the points and is ready to fight for a mate. He may round up a few yearling females, forming them into the beginnings of a harem. He may try to steal some other bull's cows. In any event, he will either challenge or be challenged by some other bull elk,

and it will be a noisy battle royal—each trying to gore his rival with his sharp antlers, both bugling their rage in voices that can be heard for miles. Sometimes the fight ends with the contestants' antlers locked.

Battle over, the winning elk retires with his wives, and they mate. (The loser may attack some weaker bull or may resign himself to being a bachelor for another year.) By then the winter is coming on fast, and it is time to hunt for warmer quarters—time to join the true herd. Leading his meek wives, the elk moves down from the upland pastures to the more protected valleys.

It is in the wintertime that elks form

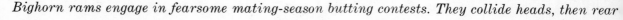

Bighorn rams engage in fearsome mating-season butting contests. They collide heads, then rear

true herds. Elk herds can be enormous. The government-protected herd in Jackson Hole, Wyoming, numbers 20,000 and would be larger if it were not kept thinned out by licensed hunting. One elk seldom has fewer than a dozen cows.

The terrible-tempered elk

Throughout the winter the bull makes himself responsible for the safety of his cows, standing off wolves and other enemies. But toward spring his antlers fall off, and that changes everything. (An elk is much easier to get along with when he has no antlers; in zoos the rack is sometimes sawed off to improve an elk's temper.) The herd breaks up. The

bulls go off together to grow new antlers, the cows go off together to have their calves. When the antlers have grown, the bull goes out once more to look for another harem.

The moose are famous for their brawls. A full-grown bull moose is large —standing 6 to 8 feet tall at the shoulder, weighing 900 to 1,500 pounds, carrying antlers 6 feet across. A timid and retiring animal most of the year, in autumn there's blood in his eye, mayhem in his heart. Snorting, stamping, bellowing, he sets out to find a female moose. When he hears a call, off he goes at full speed. (Moose calls are dismal things to human ears; many a love-sick

...ack and go at each other again and again. The one with the hardest skull is declared winner.

moose has come charging through the forest to answer the siren call of a locomotive.) Should he encounter a rival bull, the two will crash head-on, and have at one another with their 6-foot racks. Before the fight is over, they may have wrecked an entire clearing.

This is a common pattern of herd life —the members splitting up, coming together for protection and shelter, then splitting up again. American bison (the buffalo) live like this. So do many kinds of wild cattle and wild goats. Other animals form themselves into two kinds of herds, male and female, and mingle only during mating season.

Ewes of the Rocky Mountain bighorn sheep associate in herds of about twenty, led by an old matron. A ewe leader gets her position by seniority, and she keeps it until she dies.

A lamb starts out in life following its mother. The male lambs drift away when they are grown, but females remain— and continue to follow their mothers, even when they are themselves fullgrown ewes and have lambs of their own. In this way, a ewe is automatically "promoted," and if she lives long enough, she will eventually be the flock leader.

In Africa, where the climate is tropical or temperate, there is little problem

Gazelles, fastest of the antelope, are fleet enough to escape hunters they dare not fight.

The gorilla drums on his chest to warn intruders to keep away from his family.

of keeping warm or finding food. Instead, herd life revolves around two other things: finding water and escaping predators. Large herds are seldom necessary. Some antelope—duikers, for instance—travel in pairs. Others form herds that consist of one bull and a dozen cows, plus a few young bachelors. Sometimes these smaller units join with other groups and form a herd of fifty or a hundred. In some areas, two, three, or more kinds of antelope may graze beside the same water hole in a sort of composite herd.

Except for gazelles and oryxes—desert animals which can go for long spells without water—the way of life of these animals is determined by the water supply. Waterbucks are never found more than half a mile from water, and pukus and lechwes do most of their browsing in and near swampland. Impala herds travel great distances, but never leave the river valley. Others simply stay within daily reach of river or lake and go down to drink at dawn and dusk.

Home is a big place

A herd animal may have no fixed home, but that does not mean he wanders everywhere. An animal has his own territory, and he sticks to it. But it may be as large as the North Atlantic or the Sahara; it may take him days to travel from one end of his "home" to the other, and its boundaries may be determined only by vegetation or climate.

Stags spend most of the year within an area of less than a square mile. White-tailed deer also stay within a narrow "domain"—in hard times they will starve to death before moving a few miles to a food supply.

It is within this territory, whatever its size, that a nomad moves. Often he follows well-worn trails, often he tramples out trails of his own. Some animals, although sharing this area freely with animals of other species, will not tolerate those of their own kind nearby. The reason is simple: They will be competing for the same food supply and also for the same females.

59

This territorial instinct survives in pet dogs. A Chihuahua often threatens and expels a Great Dane that sets foot on *his* soil.

Headquarters for a herd of hippopotamuses is always some gently flowing river. Here they spend their days, resting and tending their young together. But after dark they move inland to roam about in search of food, each animal foraging in his own loop of land. This territory belongs to him and his mate and their young—perhaps a few cousins, too—and other hippos stay away.

Vicuñas, small cousins of the llama, live high up—12,000 to 18,000 feet—in the South American mountains, where air is thin and pastureland comparatively scarce. One mature male leads a family herd of one to nine females, plus their young. (There are also male herds made up of the too young and the too old.) This leader stations himself on a pinnacle rock and keeps a lookout—for trespassers from another herd as much as for true enemies. When he sees something, he whistles shrilly and comes leaping down, either to cover the herd's retreat or to expel the intruders.

The shy but massive gorilla does not

Musk-oxen protect themselves by forming a circle with the females and young in the middle.

like outsiders either. Too heavy to swing lightly through the trees and thus escape intruders, he keeps them at bay by making a loud fuss. First he hoots—softly in the beginning, but growing louder and louder, faster and faster. Then, standing up, he bares his gigantic chest and starts thumping. His chest is like a great drum, and the sound carries for a long way, warning other gorillas and animals of prey—and men—to keep their distance.

Seal and walrus herds have their pet breeding grounds to which they resort year after year. Not only do they return persistently to these same areas, but they often put up a battle against outsiders that try to horn in.

Herd-life etiquette

Herd life has many rules and customs. A herd is a society, and like any society, even human, the members must know how to get along with one another. Consequently, herd life develops many special ways of behaving.

One of these is rank, a system by which an individual's importance is established. Some animals, like some humans, are naturally dominant—stronger willed than others, more sure of themselves, sometimes physically stronger, sometimes more intelligent. Every animal establishes his authority over those animals which are inferior to him.

Hens work out what is called the "pecking order." Two hens meeting for the first time will peck at one another until one gives in. The loser may not be hurt at all, but merely convinced that her opponent is a more important hen than she. From then on the loser submits humbly to the winner and considers herself lower in rank. Ultimately the flock attains a very stable pecking order: Hen A can peck all the other hens; hen B can peck all the hens except A; hen C can peck all the hens except A and B, and so on. High-ranking hens eat first, gain more weight, look sleeker, lay more eggs—and, naturally, show fewer peck scars.

Cows attain their social rank by butting, but once the order is established, the discord is at an end. The head cow leads the herd when it moves to and from pasture, and is deferred to by all the others. Sometimes would-be social climbers—cows second or third in rank, but unable to out-butt the current No. 1 —are the worst-tempered animals in the herd. Most placid, after the sleek and satisfied queen, are those meek creatures at the bottom of the herd. Why should they strive? *Everybody* is better than they are!

This same system prevails among many kinds of wild animals, but is complicated by the presence of male animals. As a rule, all males rank higher than all females.

Bottle-nose dolphins live a very sheep-like pattern—separating into bull herds and getting together only during the breeding season. Apparently each group has its own social order, the dominant

Elephants are intensely loyal to their herd mates. They will rally around a sick friend to get

animals achieving their rank by nudging their comrades, lashing with their tails or simply looking tough. However, when the two groups join, the females drop their own system, and each female takes her rank from that of her mate.

The art of mutual defense

Another attribute of herd life is mutual protection. Musk-oxen protect themselves against wolves by forming a living fortress.

The musk-ox (actually not an ox at all, but a kind of goat) has horns that cover the top of his head and curve down beside his face. This "helmet" is sorely needed when hungry beasts of prey are prowling the Arctic tundra where he lives. Taking alarm, the herd forms a circle—males facing outward with heads lowered, females and young in the center. Seeing that deadly battle line of horns, the polar bear hesitates and then turns aside. The wily wolf pack can only circle the herd, howling and snapping. Few creatures, no matter how savage, make a meal of the musk-ox!

Whales, walrus and dolphins frequently offer group defense against that

him back on his feet. Even the young, usually busy with fun, will "play nurse" to a sick calf.

wolf of the sea, the killer whale. Common dolphins, finding themselves surrounded by a school of killers, form a protective shield around their young. However, they have no helmet of horns for a weapon, so some of their number are taken. They frequently push weaker members out of the circle, offering them as a kind of sacrifice for the survival of the herd as a whole.

Monkeys are very loyal companions and so are apes. Psychologists who work with chimpanzees take care not to punish one animal in the presence of others —the chimps regard the punishment as an attack on their troop mate, and they will fiercely gang up on the punisher. Captive chimps are most courageous and alert when with other chimps. In the wild, chimps are always ready to come to the assistance of a comrade in trouble. Chimpanzee troops are comparatively small, but when attacked, they yell—literally—for help, and nearby troops will rush to their aid.

Not many animals will come to the aid of an injured fellow, but those that do are herd animals. A bottle-nose dolphin in distress whistles, bringing other dolphins to his assistance. One on

Baboon societies often engage in activities very like those of human beings. Some have even been known to keep pets. Baboon children enjoy a goat-back ride as much as human children do!

either side, they boost him to the surface and keep him there until he recovers. Dolphins have been known to do this for human swimmers, too.

Gray, humpback and Greenland whales do much the same. Although surrounded by whaling ships, one whale will support another until he is wounded himself. Indeed, so strong is the whale's instinct for saving creatures that he will nudge another animal to the surface even while he himself is bleeding. A sperm whale mother will support her wounded calf in her mouth.

Another animal which gives help to his wounded comrade is the elephant. Hunter after hunter has told of seeing elephants coming staunchly to the aid of a wounded herd mate. In one case, a dozen members of a herd struggled to get a mortally wounded animal on his feet. In another, two calves, hardly more than babies, came to the aid of a third young one, which had been shot, and supported him between them until they were all back with the herd.

Dolphins, whales and elephants are among the cleverest creatures in the

Animal Kingdom. Sea lions, pigs, monkeys and apes are also highly intelligent animals—and herd dwellers. Dogs, descended from pack-living wolves, are far brighter than the solitary cats.

The ones with high I.Q.

Herd animals are quicker to learn tricks and acts for zoo or circus performances than are solitary animals. Most circus lions and tigers are limited to forming pyramids and roaring on cue. But elephants stand on their heads, play soccer, open bottles, balance on balls, ring handbells, lead parades. Chimpanzees roller-skate, ride bicycles and ponies. Dolphins toss balls through basketball hoops, play catch with their audiences and pull boats. Sea lions play tunes, and even do a kind of dance.

It is thought that herd animals regard the trainer as a member of their herd—a member with the highest rank.

Of all animal societies, perhaps the most advanced—or at least the most highly organized—is that of the baboon. The baboon is one of the very few members of the monkey family to live on the ground. He climbs trees when he needs to spy out the land, however, and his home is usually among rocky cliffs. He belongs to a tribe numbering thirty to a hundred in normal times, following a single leader.

One South African tribe of 300 baboons had eleven leaders—perhaps each one the head of a subtribe, the way a caribou buck is head of his own subherd.

These eleven leaders were large old males. They walked at the head of the tribe, "conferred" over unusual situations, growled out "orders" to retreat or advance, led the assault on tribe enemies, and got the best of the food. Fights frequently occurred among members of the tribe, but never between leader and leader or leader and member. Each leader had one mate and was faithful to her.

Baboons vary a good deal in their habits. They are usually cowardly when found alone, but in a large enough group they will raid farms, even city suburbs. They have been reported to keep pets, one tribe owning a tame goat, which they took around with them on their travels and sometimes playfully rode. They learn so fast and can adapt so well to new circumstances that in one area the animals have changed from leaf-eating herbivores to sheep-killing carnivores—all within ten years.

The skill of a circus performer

At various times, tame baboons have served man as water haulers, floor sweepers, fruit pickers, waiters, stackers of wood, garden weeders and longshoremen—jobs requiring both the skill of a circus performer and the reliability of a farm animal. It is doubtful if any creature but the baboon—clever, deft, quick to learn—could master crafts of this kind.

But if any other animal could, it would be a herd animal.

65

CHAPTER
5

Starting a Family

When it comes to disciplining the children, most animal fathers give mothers a free hand. But protecting the young is often a father's job

Next to eating, sleeping and preserving his life, an animal's strongest urge is to reproduce. Among higher animals, this means the bringing together of male and female, the establishment of a home or place where the young will be safe and provisions for their rearing to adulthood.

For birds and mammals, reproduction is a serious duty, occupying a good portion of their time and energy. It begins when a male sees a desirable female and sets his cap for her—or it may be the other way around.

The pocket gopher likes to live alone; meeting another gopher in his underground passageways, he fights him to the death. But in the spring he feels the need of company. Emerging from his burrow—something he does for no other reason and at no other time of the year —he trundles off across the prairie in search of a female gopher. She is awaiting him in her burrow; she doesn't go out to meet him, but if he finds her, she is ready. They mate, he leaves, and one month later a litter of small gophers is born in the female's burrow.

This is animal courtship at its simplest. Other males, sallying forth to woo and win, don't have things quite so easy.

The chipmunk sets out to find a mate as soon as he awakens from his winter's

66

When baby opossums are big enough to leave mother's pouch, they ride her back, clinging tightly.

sleep. He has to proceed with caution. He finds a female's burrow, but hesitates nervously before entering. Suppose this female is still hibernating? She won't like being awakened! Suppose she's too hungry or too cross or simply not in the mood to receive gentlemen callers? *Then* he'll catch it! He decides to try his luck. He creeps down the entrance tunnel until he finds her. A moment of suspense—then she accepts his timid advances.

Many males must make long journeys before they even find a female. Muskrats may travel 15 to 20 miles in search of mates. The wood rat goes out every night on half-mile trips, well beyond his usual territory. Skunks roam far and wide and so do porcupines.

In many cases, the female throws

Wood-rat courtship is a lively affair. The partners box and squeak and rub whiskers.

modesty to the winds and does the hunting herself. The female puma, for instance, leaves her kittens on their ninth day to go looking for another mate.

Females are notoriously coy

The little white-footed mouse is a flirt. She hunts for a mate, but then, having found him, pretends indifference—just long enough to get him to chase her. Caught, she does another about-face. Finally, she lures him in to her nest. But after a day or so, she throws him out.

The muskrat, even after his long journey, gets much the same treatment. First, he must chase the female—in and out of the water—then, having caught her, he will be allowed to remain only for about a week.

The wood rat has his troubles, too. When he approaches a female, she rises on her haunches and spars with him, squeaking indignantly. Tiring after a round or two, she pauses. They rest their paws on each other's shoulders and rub whiskers. Then off they go again, battling away, until finally the female's resistance is exhausted.

Not all female animals are so forward. Actually, most females are so meek and submissive that they allow the male to do all the choosing of mates. Among deer, antelope, goats, sheep—in fact, almost all herd animals—the male fights other males for possession of the female, and she is bestowed on the winner.

Male giraffes do battle with their necks, using them like clubs. First they

A male bird courts a prospective mate by bringing her nesting materials. Penguins nest in stones, so a courting penguin will drop pebbles at the feet of the lady of his choice.

face each other, head to head, each one looking out for a chance to get past the other's guard. Then one makes his move. Jerking his head out to the side, he swings it at his rival, trying to jab him in the ribs with his blunt little horns. Chances are his rival will parry the blow, and the two necks will crack together like a pair of dueling swords. Fortunately, giraffes are mild-tempered. Often enough, they both miss altogether or one off-balances the other. Or, after an exchange of mild whacks, both lose interest.

Jackrabbits, however, can be quite fierce. Rival males stand erect, facing one another, snapping and biting at each other's ears. Then they box—a rapid-fire one-two. If one sees his chance, he slashes out with his great hind feet at his rival's unprotected stomach. Mating season for jackrabbits lasts from early spring to midsummer, and by the end of it, a husky jack is bound to have quite a few scars.

Among many animals, these battles are only a form. Some antelope and even deer make only the most delicate and harmless passes at one another with their horns. Fallow deer will march side by side, then pause and make careful passes at one another. Chivalrously, neither takes advantage of any mistakes that might be made by his opponent.

69

All this scrapping and bickering—the battles between rival males for possession of a harem, squabblings between mates before the female gives in—all this work is for the good of the species in general. For it guarantees that the strongest, the cleverest animals father the greatest number of children.

Still, courtship among animals is not all battle. Some partners show great tenderness toward one another, others are so full of delight that they burst into boisterous romping.

The bear and the porcupine—two unlikely looking Romeos—shed their customary aloofness at mating time and turn exceedingly affectionate. So do elephants. An elephant romance may last for months, and while it is on, the courting couple is constantly together, feeding one another choice tidbits, entwining trunks, taking playful nips or pokes.

Some sing at mating time

Mice often "sing" at mating time. The harvest mouse has two mating seasons a year, one in autumn, one in spring. At those times he runs about fluting in an extremely high pitch, quite different from his usual sound.

Birds do not necessarily rely on song to do all their wooing and winning. It is common for a courting male to bring his prospective bride gifts of straw or twigs—nesting materials. The penguin cannot sing at all; he drops a pebble at the feet of his chosen mate—penguins make their nests of pebbles. If she is willing to accept him, she picks it up.

The hummingbird shows off his flying ability to the mate he is courting, moving back and forth in front of her in an arc, pendulum-fashion. The daredevil roller bird of West Africa does a breakneck dive. Flying up to a dizzy height, he half folds his wings and lets himself fall—tumbling head over heels, rolling about from one side to the other, finally catching himself in the nick of time.

Some "square dance"

Skunks are by nature good-tempered and affectionate creatures—understandably, since their defensive weapons make them all but immune to attack. The males fight over the females, but once a couple has paired off, their courtship turns into a kind of dance. She opens the proceedings by strutting in front of him with arched back, while he patters his feet and works up an excited chattering. Then, drawing apart, the pair face each other and begin a stiff-legged advance and retreat—bounce forward, touch noses, bounce back, and repeat—like two Virginia Reelers.

The mating dance of the cottontails is more like a game of leapfrog. Taking turns, male and female leap into the air —one bouncing straight up while the other dashes underneath.

Humpback whales carry on what must be the most rollicking courtship in the world. A bull humpback, out to impress a female, may stand on his head in the water—one-third of him sticking out—

and waggle his flukes (the pointed ends of his tail). Or he may charge up to the surface, burst through it until all 75 tons of him are clear of the water, and then fall back with a splash that almost raises a tidal wave. Or he may pummel her with his great flipper and get pummeled in return—playful blows, but heard for miles.

Having found, courted and won his mate, a male animal usually feels that his duty is done—the babies and their care are no concern of his! Off he goes.

The mother's first job is to prepare for the birth of her young. If she has a permanent burrow, she cleans it out, brings in new bedding, possibly remodels the nesting chamber. Or she digs a special room in which to keep the new brood, perhaps sealing off the old chambers. Or it may be her habit to dig an entirely fresh burrow or weave a brand new nest.

If the mother-to-be is a herd animal, she will separate from the group a few days before the babies are due and go off to some sheltered grove of trees. Sometimes, several prospective mothers retire together and form a kind of maternity ward. Dholes, wild dogs of India, which live in rocky areas, often set aside a special cave for the exclusive

Cottontail rabbits have a kind of mating game. The partners play leapfrog and tag, first one in the lead and then the other. This gay courtship game may well go on all night long.

The little hopping kangaroo rat of the deserts is a loyal mother. If an enemy invades her burrow, she may flee to safety with her babies in her arms—much like a human mother.

use of mothers and puppies. Cape hunting dogs dig out old aardvark nests, line them with fresh bedding, and establish all the mother dogs inside.

An elephant makes careful preparation for the birth of her child. First she chooses a female friend (nicknamed an "auntie" by Burmese elephant herders) to help her. This is usually an older and more experienced animal. Together, mother-to-be and auntie choose a place— an open spot well screened with shrubbery is preferred—and clear it off carefully. The herd waits far enough away to give the mother privacy, but close

enough to come to her aid if there should be any tigers in the area.

After the baby comes, the auntie stands guard while the mother cleans off the calf's woolly, 3-foot-tall body and gets him onto his feet. At the end of two days, he is able to travel, and the three rejoin the herd. Mother and auntie remain with the calf continuously for the next few weeks. They keep him between them at moments of danger, they feed on either side of him, they help him across the streams and through swamps by clasping trunks under his belly. When the herd is attacked, the aunties often hustle the babies away while the mothers scatter the enemy.

Once the young of any animal are safely born, the mother has the twin problems of feeding and protecting them. For their first few weeks of life, new-born mammals subsist on milk supplied by the mother's own body. This means that in order to feed her young a mother mammal must feed herself.

Some animals are able to store up special reserves within their bodies to carry them past the crucial nursing period. Bears have it easy. Their young are born in winter while the mother is still in a state of semihibernation. The babies nurse while she sleeps, and by the time spring arrives, they are big enough to go out foraging with her.

A shrew family travels in a living chain, tail of one held in the mouth of the next.

Gray seals of the North Atlantic and monk seals of the mid-Pacific become enormously fat just before the birth of their pups. They come ashore to give birth and then remain on shore, without eating food of any kind, until the pups are weaned. For gray seals, this means a period of three weeks; for monk seals, five weeks. A nursing mother may lose more than one-third of her body weight before her pup can fend for himself.

Life is filled with danger

But more commonly, the mothers have to eat during the nursing period, and this usually means they must leave the babies for a while every day. Often their anxiety to get home makes them bold, forgetful of precautions. Wolf mothers, heading for their dens, make tracks as straight as an arrow, whereas their heading-out tracks meander. Other mothers take precautions, too.

Life is dangerous for young mammals. Only one-third of a litter of woodchucks survives for a full year—and only seven out of ten cottontails. Even among tigers, half or more of a litter will die before its first birthday.

A muskrat family, flooded out of its watery home, is carried to safety in its mother's mouth. It is said that a kangaroo rat, her desert burrow invaded by a badger, will hop away in terror with her arms full of babies.

When danger threatens the common shrew and her brood, they form a living chain—Baby No. 1 clutching the fur at

73

the base of his mother's tail with his teeth, Baby No. 2 attached to Baby No. 1 and so on. The mother drags them all to safety.

Pouched animals, such as the kangaroo, the wombat, the opossum, have built-in pockets in which to carry their young. When baby opossums grow too big for their mother's pouch, they ride on her back, clinging to her fur. The problems of protection and feeding are both solved if the young can be carried along with the mother wherever she goes. Baby monkeys are born with the ability to cling, and support their own weight. An infant chimpanzee, orangutan or gibbon clings to his mother's thighs while she swings through the trees by her hands; her tucked-up legs act as a kind of catch basket or safety net in case he loses his grip.

Some animal mothers, needing to be away from their youngsters for a while, call in a baby-sitter. A lone female giraffe is frequently left to watch out over a herd of babies and half-grown animals. The manatee has often been seen holding her own baby in one flipper, her neighbor's in the other.

Some make good fathers

Although many male animals disappear when mating is over, some stay around to be useful in raising the young.

After the female Adélie penguin has laid her regulation two eggs, she is off for the sea. Her mate stays meekly behind, brooding the eggs, until she returns to relieve him, two weeks later. Then it is his turn to go off to the sea, leaving her with the eggs. They alternate for two months until the eggs are hatched. The bird that is brooding the eggs gets nothing to eat, because penguins eat only fish and the nesting site is far inland.

Father carries the babies

This is quite a high standard of fatherhood, but many other animals can match it. The marmosets, for instance. The marmosets of South America, distant relatives of monkeys and apes, live in the trees, leaping from branch to branch and scampering from one precarious limb to the next. Through all this, it is the father that carries the babies—usually two at a time. They cling to his back, either one above the other or one on each hip, and he only brings them to their mother when it is time for food.

When a female baboon is about to have her baby, she and her mate retire to a secluded spot—sometimes the same spot used by all mothers in the tribe—and he keeps intruders away while she is giving birth. They will permit no one to touch their newborn baby except his older brothers and sisters, which are allowed to smell and finger him all over and thus "learn" him. While he is tiny, he clings to his mother's chest fur; later he moves around to her back. When danger threatens or there is a difficult part of trail to pass, the father carries the baby until the trouble is over.

In marmoset families, the father frequently carries the babies, sometimes two at a time.

Famed for his slyness and sharp wits, the fox never hunts near home. He does not want to advertise the presence of his den. Often he will travel 2 or 3 miles to catch dinner for his hungry dependents, rather than take advantage of nearby prey. And should a wolverine or a puma, a wolf or a bear—or a man—come hunting him, the fox will lead his enemy a merry chase in a direction away from his den. Indeed, if necessary, he will give up his life for his mate and their helpless young.

The lowly platypus of Australia takes no active part in rearing his young, but he does stick around. Male and female live together throughout most of the year. Their courtship begins at the end

of the short Australian winter. The male seizes the female's tail in his leathery beak and they swim around in circles. Then the female goes off by herself to dig a special nursery burrow and lay her eggs—the platypus is the only mammal that lays eggs.

When the eggs are hatched, the mother unplugs her burrow and goes in search of food. But not until the babies are weaned—four months later—does she take her children to live with their father. They move back to the home burrow, where the father has been placidly living alone all this time.

Two creatures from opposite sides of the world may be named as good fathers—surprisingly so, considering the

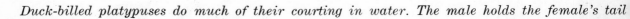

Duck-billed platypuses do much of their courting in water. The male holds the female's tail

animal clans to which they belong. One is the jaguar. Most male cats walk off and leave the female to raise the kittens —if they don't actually kill their own offspring out of jealousy. But the jaguar stays around and helps.

Like other big cats, jaguars have a loving and romantic courtship. They lick one another's fur, rub together. The male will fight to protect his mate and their young. He will hunt for them. He will sometimes even take part in their training—normally a job reserved for the animals' mother. Even after the kittens are old enough to be on their own, and depart to live their own lives, the jaguar is apt to remain with his mate. They may have another litter or several

—and they may remain mates for life.

The other good animal father is the lesser panda—a woolly little inhabitant of Asia, which looks more like his distant cousin, the raccoon, than like his close relative, the giant panda. This same raccoon and also the coatimundi, the cacomistle, the kinkajou and other assorted American relatives are all happy-go-lucky, love-'em-and-leave-'em parents; so are bears, also distant relatives. But the lesser panda mates for life and is seldom seen without his spouse.

Thus each animal, in his own way, brings new life into the world, nourishes and protects it, and sends it forth to keep the earth populated.

n his leathery beak and they swim in circles. The female lays her eggs in a nursery burrow.

CHAPTER

6

Bringing Up Baby

For young animals, play time is a time for learning—how to find dinner, how to make a comfortable bed, even how to stay alive, begin as games

78

The newly born mammal is not only too weak to take care of himself, he is also too ignorant. In his short childhood, he must learn many lessons. Some of them his mother teaches him; some he teaches himself. How well he does in "school" often determines how much he gets to eat, how big he grows and how long he lives.

It is a warm June night, and a mother hedgehog is conducting her first class in a course that might be called How a Small Animal Stays Alive. Her pupils are her five babies, just four weeks old. The tiny spines all over their backs have hardened, so they are ready to emerge from their nest under a fallen log and take a look at the outside world. Their mother raises her head and sniffs...listens...looks around. So far, so good. She takes a few steps, then something alarms her.

With a curious little leap, she pulls her head and feet together and snaps into a ball. Her delicate nose and unprotected legs are tucked under her, while from every part of her exposed back protrude sharp spines. The enemy that tries to seize her—and most animals know better—will only get a mouthful of prickles.

The little hedgehogs mimic their mother, and they too are safe. They

Small hedgehogs learn survival technique from their mother: roll up into an unappetizing ball.

The armadillo's back wears a coat of armor. When threatened, he curls up—hard side out.

have learned that a hedgehog, too weak to fight back, can stay alive if he makes himself proof against attack.

That is the first and most important lesson every young animal must learn—how to keep from getting killed.

Armadillos and pangolins both wear a kind of natural armor. Neither is helpless, having stout claws on all four feet, but they are peace-loving animals, and when threatened will curl up like the hedgehog.

The three-banded armadillo, living in Argentina, is so constructed that he can close himself up completely, like a clamshell. The little opening in the front of the shell is plugged by the animal's armor-plated head and tail, the two pieces fitting together exactly.

Porcupines make a more spirited defense than either hedgehogs or the armored animals—and so they should, for they are well-equipped to fend off attackers. Porcupines not only have spines, but quills as well. Spines are merely modified hairs, extremely stiff and prickly, but thin. Quills are thick; their tips are sharp. Furthermore, they are attached to the porcupine's skin very loosely and when touched, they pull out —usually sticking tight in the skin of the toucher.

The quills of the North American porcupine, in addition to being sharp, are barbed. These barbed quills work rather like miniature harpoons. A moment after the quill is imbedded, the tiny barbs rise and lock the quill in place. It can then be removed only by a human being. The wild animal that gets impaled with porcupine quills carries them until his death.

Many of these forms of defense are instinctive. Small skunks try to spray long before they are old enough to have acquired an adult supply of butyl mercaptan, the foul-smelling acid which skunks discharge when alarmed. But if the mother animal does not have to teach her young *what* to do, she often does have to teach them *when* to do it.

A mother raccoon is strolling through the forest, followed in single file by her brood of four. They are a full two months old, and this is their first time of being at large in the woods. If their noses catch a strange scent, they do not connect it with danger. But their mother does. That smell is dog. In a flash, the mother has shooed her young ones up a tree. If they hesitate or refuse, she clouts them sharply to teach obedience. Then she leads her enemy away.

What does danger smell like?

When the mother raccoon knows that her enemy is no longer on her trail, she returns to her babies. They have learned that danger smells like a dog.

An adult bear has few enemies, but her babies are considered fair game by pumas, wolves, wolverines and other large predators. Like the mother raccoon, a mother bear shoos her young up a tree at the first hint of danger, cuffs them if they disobey, and does not let them down until she is sure that it is safe. The mother bear also sends her cubs scooting up a tree when she feels like a nap; tired of waiting, they frequently waken her with their plaintive pleas for permission to come down again.

A safe, snug pouch

The lesser anteater often does not wait for danger, but simply puts her youngsters up in a tree and leaves them there for safekeeping all day. Koalas, bear-like marsupials of Australia, are tree-dwelling animals by nature, but the babies are a year or more old before they learn to climb for themselves. Their first three months are spent in their mother's pouch, the next nine on her back. Sometimes they are as big as she is before they go off on their own.

Although affectionate and long-suffering, a mother koala can be tried too far. When that happens, she turns junior over her knee and applies the flat of her hand to the seat of his pants.

Many young animals are taught to stand completely still at the smell or sight of danger, in hopes of becoming invisible. The European rabbit teaches her babies that, when threatened, they must flatten out on the ground, where their brownish-whittish coloring will blend with the grass and shrubbery. Sloths, when motionless, are either quite invisible or easily mistaken for something else—a bird's nest, a cluster of flowers, a termite's nest. The three-toed variety is particularly hard to spot in its tree home, since its fur frequently becomes covered with a minute plant life called algae, turning the animal green.

Lie absolutely still!

Lambs and kids begin to follow at their mothers' sides on the day of their birth. But young deer spend their first few days hidden in some quiet thicket, while their mothers wander off to browse, usually returning to nurse at dawn and dusk. Most fawns (moose calves are an exception) are born with a dappled coat, which blends well with the filtered sunlight of the woods. But movement would spoil the effect, so a fawn must learn to lie absolutely still.

The urge to follow is instinctive in many herd animals. Caribou calves which were banded by a team of Alaskan students often refused to return to the herd, preferring to follow their banders with embarrassing affection.

The great Indian (one-horned) rhinoceros seems to reverse this baby-follow-mother technique, however. The baby goes first, the mother immediately behind. She keeps the tip of her single horn just behind his rump, where she is in a good position to give him a poke if he should loiter at the wrong moment.

In addition to showing their young what to do and when to do it, many animal mothers give them examples of magnificent courage and maternal affection. As a rule, the gentle giraffe knows only one thing to do at a time of danger: run. But when she has a helpless calf, a giraffe mother will stand her ground against a lion. Equally courageous, female white-tailed deer have been known to trample rattlesnakes and even coyotes, while a female elk can tree a full-grown bear.

But just being safe is not enough. A young animal must also learn how to get his food, how to run and leap and find his way, how to swim or climb or fly or perform whatever other specialties his future way of life will require. Many of these skills come through instinct. But many must be learned anew with each generation. Indeed, the cleverer, the more versatile an animal breed, the more there is for him to learn. Hunting techniques are developed in young animals by imitation of their mothers.

The leopard is only the fifth biggest cat in the world, but he is probably the most deeply feared animal of all, for no creature surpasses him in strength and courage—and cunning.

It is the leopard's cunning that makes him so efficient a hunter. He moves through the forest with such speed and silence that few people have ever caught more than a flashing glimpse of him. He seems to develop a particular technique for every occasion.

The leopard is a learner, adapting his hunting method to the ways of his prey. The wilier he is—and the more he learns

When young, grizzly bears can climb trees. Their mother will send them aloft if danger is near—or when she wants to take a nap. Bored, they plead to be allowed to come down.

from his mother and from experience—the longer and the better he will live.

Entirely different is the life of a young skunk. He learns early that his curious weapon, the built-in spray gun, gives him a certain amount of security. When he is five weeks old, his mother takes him out on his first foraging expedition. As she sallies forth, he and his brothers and sisters—five or six of them—fall into single file behind her. She ambles along confidently, turning over stones in her hunt for termites and grubs, showing the little ones where to

find frogs and minnows, turtle eggs, beetles. Then they meet a prowling fisher—the second biggest member of the weasel family, a deadly hunter, and three times the size of the mother skunk.

Mother skunk stops and glares. Fisher hesitates. She stamps her feet threateningly and then turns and raises her plume-like tail. That does it—the fisher vanishes. The mother skunk lowers her tail and calmly marshals her little class into order once again.

Among European badgers—those home-loving, family-minded creatures—

even the father pitches in to do some guiding of the young. The cubs are born in early spring, and when they are a few weeks old, they begin to nag their parents with shrill and plaintive squeaks to be allowed out. But the sow (female) and the boar (male) do not permit themselves to be hurried. It is usually June before the big night comes.

The boar emerges first, sniffs all around, and then sits down to have a good scratch, meanwhile taking a careful look in all directions. When he is satisfied, it is the sow's turn. She is even more careful than her mate. A good sniff, a scratch, a careful look up this path and that—and at long last she moves out of the tunnel entrance and lets her cubs emerge.

At first the cubs are permitted to scamper and romp nearby, sniffing, exploring, getting acquainted with the thousands of sights and smells and sounds that make up a badger's view of the world. But soon the serious business of learning the family trade begins. With the boar in the lead and the sow following, to keep an anxious eye on her happy-go-lucky offspring, they set off to dig up earthworms, locate apples or acorns, unearth a mole or rabbit, find snails or berries or frogs or mice or beechnuts or any of the dozens of other items on the badger menu.

Young ratels, or honey badgers, of Africa have a special lesson to learn: that the cry of a certain bird means that dessert is at hand. The bird is called the honey guide because he leads the ratel—and men, too—to bees' nests. Discovering a nest, he starts crying out in a high-pitched note and keeps it up until a ratel appears and breaks into the nest. The ratel carries off chunks of honeycomb; holding them between his front paws, he stretches out luxuriously on the ground and eats them. The bird gets to share what is left of the feast.

Learning a specialty

An animal's specialty must often be learned. Young deer are clumsy leapers; young giraffes don't know what to do with their legs; hunting dogs need lots of practice before they learn the meaning of what they smell. Young beavers know that they want to build dams, but their first efforts are often crude and inept. And seals, walrus otters, sea otters, hippopotamuses—and many other animals which spend more time in water than on land—must be taught to swim. Indeed, their mothers sometimes must resort to force to get them into the water.

Baby river otters are reluctant to venture into the water. Their mother tries wheedling first, then takes them for rides through the water on her back. Finally, when they least expect it, she slips out from under them. Sputtering and squeaking indignantly, they dog-paddle to the shore—and before they get there, chances are that they will have decided that they like the water after all.

With seals it takes a little longer.

They start learning to swim long before they are weaned. The usual procedure is for the mother seal to push or pull her calf into the surf and let him roll in the wash. Chances are he is alarmed and he struggles frantically to return to the nice dry beach. But soon he grows to love the feel of the water.

The hippopotamus's swimming is more like walking—indeed, as often as not, he "swims" by simply walking along the bottom—but a baby hippo must master the art just the same. While he is still small, he rides on his mother's back in deep water and stands in shallow water to nurse. But with a little training, he learns to submerge and remain below for several minutes or to lie at the surface in blissful ease.

Curiously enough, many animals that seldom swim—and even then only when pressed by an emergency—need no lessons whatsoever, but strike out naturally the first time they hit the water.

Some cats like to swim

All dogs can swim. Cats are natural swimmers, and the tiger, jaguar and fishing cat of Asia like it. Deer, antelope, horses and cows are natural swimmers, as are monkeys. Elephants can swim, but when possible, they prefer to walk on the bottom, using their trunks as snorkels (air hoses to the surface).

Flying and gliding are not, apparently, inborn gifts either, but take practice. Baby bats cling to their mothers for the first three or four days of their lives,

Most predators—like the fisher—fear the skunk's acid spray, leave him unmolested.

85

Most elephants swim if they have to, but they don't like it. They prefer to cross a river by

hooked to the fur of her body. Their father has gone off to join an all-male colony, probably in some other cave. Their mother takes them with her when she goes out to feed and brings them back at dawn to the roost. Then, when they are old enough to be left alone all day, she hangs them up in the roost and goes off foraging on her own. Finally, by the end of three weeks or so, the membranes of their wings are strong enough for them to attempt flight, and there are short trial runs for the youngsters. Probably a month after birth the young ones are full-fledged members of

the big colony of cave-dwelling bats.

Apes and monkeys have several different methods of traveling through the trees. For apes the usual method is hand over hand. Gibbons are the great athletes among the apes. They swing from branch to branch, from tree to tree, in trapeze-artist leaps—sometimes clearing a distance of 20 feet. Orangutans, considerably bigger, heavier and less agile, go hand over hand with care, testing the strength of a branch before entrusting their weight to it.

The long-tailed monkeys of Africa travel by leaps. Arms and legs out-

walking the bottom. If they wade in over their heads, their trunks serve as built-in snorkels.

spread, tails steering, they launch themselves into the air, heading for the massed leaves and branches of a nearby tree. Landing, they clutch at the foliage with hands and feet and then scramble to a place of safety.

Young monkeys are part of this tree-top life from their birth, their ability to grasp and cling being inborn. Clutching his mother's fur while she leaps or swings along, a youngster soon picks up the rhythm of monkey travel. When his little limbs are strong enough to support him, he takes his first short leaps, while the mother stands by. Soon he is

swinging along like an old veteran.

When animals are not busy mastering the business of living, what are they doing? Probably playing. And perhaps it is in their games that they do the most learning of all.

Almost all young animals engage in games to see which can run fastest or leap highest or turn quickest.

Red-deer calves play a kind of king-of-the-castle, in which one youngster takes position on a little hill and then tries to maintain it while his playmates try to shove him off. Other herd animals play follow-the-leader. Kids and lambs

87

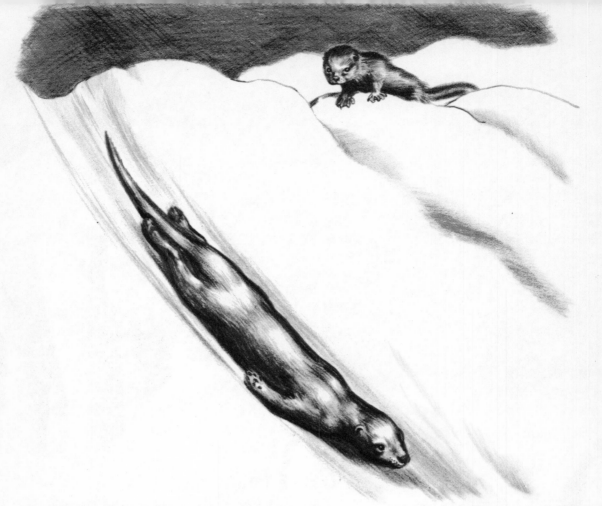

Playful otters love to slide—on mud banks in summer and on snow-covered slopes in winter.

butt each other playfully all over their pastures. Colts hold mock races. Young squirrels chase each other endlessly up one tree and down another.

Sea mammals are great funsters. Porpoises and dolphins love to follow ships, to swim around and around the slow ones and sport in the bow waves of the fast ones. Humpback whales can make the sea turbulent with their rowdy clappings. Gray whales romp in the surf and ride breakers.

Mock fighting is another kind of animal play. Bear cubs are ferocious little balls of fur, rolling and tumbling and industriously chewing on one another. If their fur were not so thick, and their baby teeth so small, fewer little bears

might live to grow up into big bears.

Mice don't wrestle—they box. So do male kangaroos, going at it in fairly regular rounds. Squaring off, two of them grapple and cuff one another with their short forepaws, leaning back on their tails and kicking out with their mighty hind feet. After about three minutes of this, they rest and then renew the battle.

In his serious moments, no animal is more intent on business than the weasel. But his hunting zeal is equaled by his zest for relaxing. Often several join in a romp, rolling one another over, twisting, turning, sparring, leaping—a 12-inch weasel can jump 4 feet into the air and turn a flying somersault.

The young of hunting animals start practicing the trade when they are barely able to walk. Kittens use their mother's tail for pouncing practice—all kittens, from those of the 13-foot Siberian tiger to those of the sleek Siamese pet. While the mother lies stretched out, languidly moving her tail from side to side, the kittens fling themselves at it. If they catch it, they hug it with their forepaws, bite it, try to stop it from moving. If they miss, they have another try. All this is their way of learning how to pounce on a moving victim.

Toys in the nursery

Many animals actually have playthings. House cats and puppies are often given corks, bits of string, old slippers to play with, but wild animals sometimes make their own. The young calves of an elephant herd in India sometimes make great balls of mud, which they roll back and forth among themselves, playing a kind of pachyderm soccer.

Most of these games are methods of learning, of sharpening the skills the animal will need in later life. But not all of them. Consider the otters, river and sea. They play their whole lives through—with delight and high spirits and with no reason except pure fun.

In the water, the river otter will play with anything he doesn't want to eat—a log, a fish, a stone. Encountering beavers or other animals too big to overcome, he will tease them—duck them, swim over and under and around them,

then dart away. If the otter has company of his own kind, he will make a slide on the bank of a stream. Finding a fairly rock-free place, one otter after another will slide down it on his chest. They go slowly at first, until the dampness of their bodies has turned the dirt to mud, and the constant sliding has made it slick. Then the sliding becomes faster and faster. Pressing his front feet to his side, the otter skims down the slope and dives into the pond. Then out of the water, a scramble up the bank, and he is ready for another turn.

In winter these slides are made on the snow, and if the otters are lucky, the river will be frozen, giving them a long "sleigh ride." Their cousins, the minks, enjoy sliding, too, but alone—quite different from the joyous sliding parties of the otter.

The sea otter spends almost his entire life in the water, coming to land only when the sea is excessively rough. When he is trying to make speed, he swims on his stomach, propelling himself by his feet. But most of the time he simply floats on his back. He eats lying on his back, using his chest as a table; he cracks clamshells on a piece of rock and lays the pieces out on his chest. He sleeps lying on his back.

But a life of leisure is only for otters. Other animals—and that includes human beings—can only sport from time to time, when they have been fed and have finished their chores for the day— when they are safe and free.

CHAPTER

7

The Well-Dressed Animal

What animal has a built-in comb? What prefers bathing in a big, sloppy mud puddle? And what takes a bath by rolling in the dust?

90

An animal does not choose his body covering, but he makes the best possible use of the one with which he was born. And so he should, for it is his protection from the rain and the cold, his insulation against the heat, a shield between him and his enemies, and often a cloak of invisibility when he walks around.

In fact, if an animal could choose his own coat, chances are that he would pick the very kind of skin or fur or shell which nature has chosen for him.

All mammals have hair, but not all have fur. Fur is a fine, short, soft, often silky coat of hair growing densely thick and close to the skin. It is interdispersed with guard hairs—true hairs, like those on human heads, much longer and coarser than fur. Since there are muscles in this deep layer of skin, the guard hairs can be raised straight up, perpendicular to the skin. When a dog "raises his hackles," he is simply tensing the guard hairs on his neck and back. The same is true of an angry and bristling cat. This hackle-raising sometimes helps discourage a would-be attacker, because when a threatened animal fluffs up, he looks bigger.

The guard hairs protect the fur from matting, from being too easily torn out or snarled. Most important of all, they form a protective covering that traps

With his tough hide and massive weapon on his nose, the rhinoceros can scatter almost any enemy.

air inside the close-growing layer of fur. The farther north an animal lives, the heavier his coat of hair.

Protected by this outer covering, some birds and mammals make their homes in places of devastating cold. The Arctic fox roams happily in temperatures many degrees below zero. Penguins cavort merrily throughout the Antarctic winter and swim in the icy water.

At the other extreme, fur and feathers not only shield an animal from the worst rays of the sun, but they allow him to shed the heat he has accumulated around his body. Birds ruffle their feathers. Mammals perspire or pant.

A warm fur coat

Fur has always been of great interest to man, and for its sake he has trapped and hunted many animals relentlessly. What makes a pelt valuable is usually the thickness and softness of the under fur. Most sought-after fur bearers live in cold climates and are comparatively small animals. They are either carnivores (ermine, marten, mink, otter, sable, raccoon, certain kinds of fox) or rodents (beaver, chinchilla, muskrat, nutria and sometimes squirrel).

In place of extra-thick under fur, some large animals have extra-long guard hairs. The musk-ox wears a kind of hula skirt that barely clears his ankles. The yak of Tibet has a cape of hair that actually sweeps the ground; additional tassels of hair cover his eyes and ears. In winter, horses grow a coat

of hair, not fur. The American bison sports a heavy mane on his head, chest and shoulders; thus protected, he prefers to meet wind and snow head on rather than turn his back to them as most animals do.

When fur is curly and has few guard hairs—particularly if the individual fur hairs are covered with microscopic scales and thus mat up easily to form felt—it is called "wool." Sheep are the principal bearers of wool. Domestic breeds have been developed which grow almost no guard hairs at all; their coats of solid wool are called "fleeces." So dense and even are the fleeces of some breeds, such as the Romney Marsh and the Cheviot, that the sheep look like walking hedges.

New clothes every year

Two kinds of goats have often been domesticated for their fine wool, which is often superior to that of sheep—the Angora goat and the Cashmere (or Kashmir) goat, both of which originated in the mountains of Asia. Unlike domestic sheep, goats do have guard hairs. In the Angora goat, these guard hairs fall out every spring—they "shed" as a dog or cat sheds—if the animals are not sheared by their masters. They grow new coats of hair every year. The Cashmere goat, however, does not lose his silky topcoat and is never sheared. It is the under wool that is wanted, and this is obtained by combing the animal.

Karakul sheep are not bred for their wool (Astrakhan), but for the hides of their lambs. The adults of this breed are various shades of brown, black and gray, but the lambs are born with a pure-black fleece of exceptional softness and delicate curl. These skins become "Persian lamb"—not a true fur, but a wool.

Other wool bearers are the camel and his distant relatives, the alpaca and the vicuña of South America. There are no wool-bearing camels specially bred for their fleeces. Camel's hair comes from ordinary, load-carrying caravan animals, and although Bactrian (two-hump) camels grow a somewhat longer wool than do dromedaries (one hump), that is only because they come from the cold mountains of Persia instead of the warm deserts of Arabia.

Camels are never sheared. In spring and early summer, when they are shedding their winter coats, their owners follow them around and pick up the bunches of shed wool as they drop. Camel caravans assign one man to bring up the rear of the procession and collect what has been shed by the whole train. These droppings of wool are then sold in the nearest city. Real camel's hair is never in large supply. To make cloth, most camel's hair is blended in the weaving with sheep's wool.

Protected by their heavy manes, a mother bison and her calf can face prairie blizzards head on.

Most mammals wear drab coats, but male mandrills are decked in bright reds, yellows, blues.

In contrast to their fur, their wool, or their hair, few animals are bred for the sake of their hides—that is for leather. Some alligators are raised on farms, destined to end up as alligator bags, and there is some trade in such exotic hides as kangaroo and pinto pony.

Some animals have exceedingly fine and delicate skins. The skin of most whales is as thin as paper, hardly more than a fragile container for the thick layers of blubber which enclose the bodies of these great animals. The smaller sea mammals—dolphins, porpoises and white whales—however, have very tough and leathery hides.

A mouthful of nothing

Some animals have very loose skins—an excellent defensive device, for when their enemies bite, they usually end up with nothing but a mouthful of skin. Badgers are loose-skinned and so, of course, are various breeds of hound.

Elephants and rhinoceroses are sometimes called "pachyderms," which means "loose-skinned animals." The hide of the great Indian rhino fits over his shoulders and hips in permanent folds; it is so tough that he looks as if he had been armor-plated. The rhinoceroses of Africa do not have these folds, but their hides are just as tough—native hunters make shields of rhino hide.

The tapirs of Central and South America are also equipped with tough hides—and a good thing, too, for these primitive and single-minded creatures spend much of their time breaking trail through the jungles.

A water-loving animal, the tapir sometimes wanders far from his native river system and must then find another one. He finds it by the most direct possible route. Often this means charging head on through tangled undergrowth and shrubbery, but the tapir's hide is proof against a few scratches and scrapes. He usually leaves behind him a route that's worth following—indeed, some Central American highways owe their present locations to old tapir paths.

A most delicate complexion

By contrast, the hippopotamus has an exceedingly delicate complexion, even though his skin is an inch or more thick. It is full of pores and rather sponge-like in its ability to absorb water. If it is not kept wet, it will dry up and crack. The hippo spends most of his waking hours in the water. But when he must be ashore, his skin glands give off a greasy pink substance, which protects his hide until he returns to his river home.

Compared with reptiles, fish, amphibians, and especially birds—many of whom are garbed from nose to tail in the brightest of colors—mammals are Quakers. A mammal's coat is usually gray or black or brown or yellow or tan or white, or a combination of these colors. It is useful for him to be garbed unobtrusively.

Poisonous reptiles are often brightly colored, like the red, yellow and black-

Many jungle cats, such as the ocelot, wear spotted or striped coats. In the shadowy forest world, this exotic pattern—blending in with the background—makes the animals almost invisible.

ringed coral snake. It is as though a bright coat serves as a warning. The Gila monster, America's only poisonous lizard, is spotted all over with blotches of pink or orange and black.

Or bright colors can mean that an animal isn't very good to eat. The tiny hummingbirds are abroad in daylight, flashing their brilliant plumage wherever they choose, but birds of prey leave them strictly alone.

Sometimes bright colors are only a means of mimicking another animal, perhaps taking advantage of his immunity to attack. The scarlet snake and the scarlet king snakes, both nonven-

omus, look so much like the deadly coral snake that they can command a good deal of unearned respect.

Different colors for different sexes is most common among birds, but some members of the monkey family have these color differences, too. A male mandrill sports a bright rose-colored nose, a pale yellow beard, and baby-blue cheeks, and the color scheme is carried through and harmonized with his posterior. His bride, although fairly colorful, cannot begin to match him.

But bright colors are decidedly rare among animals. Whether he is the hunted or the hunter, a mammal benefits by being hard to see, so his colors usually blend with his natural background. Colors and markings that help an animal to hide are called "procryptic coloration."

For many animals, the most useful procryptic coloration is simply a plain coat of dull color with very little marking. Such a coat will blend equally well with dusty ground, trunks of trees, ripening stalks of grass. This is called "general procryptic coloration." An animal with this kind of coat is not absolutely invisible anywhere, but he is generally a little hard to see everywhere. Most animals throughout the world have general procryptic coloration.

Exotic patterns and color schemes

But others—notably antelope, the great cats, the young of the deer family, and black-and-white animals—have "special procryptic coloration." This works in quite the opposite way. These animals have coats of an exotic pattern and color scheme designed to make them almost invisible, but only in one particular area. In a zoo, a zebra's convict stripes may be plainly seen many yards away, but in his native forest's sun-and-shade pattern, he vanishes.

Most members of the Animal Kingdom see very poorly. Aside from certain insects (among them bees), it is believed that the only animals with color vision are birds and some members of the monkey family. Other animals seem to see only in a shadowy way. They can-

not detect depth well, but they can pick out certain lines and patterns, and they can tell when those patterns are interrupted or broken—as, for example, when a solid-colored animal places himself in front of a background of leaves. And, of course, if the break-in-the-pattern moves, then the viewer knows another animal is present.

Special procryptic coloration does two things: It breaks up the pattern of the animal, and it continues the pattern of the background. When an okapi stands still, his loud stripes no longer outline his hind quarters—they form part of the

Monkeys like to groom one another, picking off and eating tiny flakes of salty skin.

streaks of sunlight falling across the jungle floor. Most elaborately decorated of all are the jungle cats—the tiger with his handsome stripes, and the jaguar, the cheetah, the serval, the margay and the ocelot, all with spots and speckles. The jungles and forests of the world are also full of smaller spotted members of the cat family. Indeed, the young of some non-spotted cats are born with spots—the lion, the lynx and the pumas —and these spots do not disappear until the kittens are old enough to need no further concealment.

It is so useful for an animal to blend into his background that nature sometimes allows him to change color. Chameleons vary the shade of their skin according to the temperature and light intensity of their surroundings.

There are no quick-change artists among the mammals, but some of them do undergo slower and more gradual changes in color. Very marked changes take place in the fur of some seals. Harp seals, born on pack ice, are pure white at birth. By the age of four weeks, when they start learning to swim, they have grown a coat of pale, deep-sea gray. The animals' coats continue to pass through several color changes until they are full grown, at age four or five, when they settle down with light gray or ivory pelts, marked on the back with a brown circle or "harp."

Another kind of color change takes place with the seasons. The weasel changes to white when winter comes—

all but the tip of his tail, which remains black all year around. In one way, winter garb is rather unfortunate for the weasel—in white he is known as the ermine, and his beautiful fur, once used to trim the court robes of kings, is in great demand. The fur itself never changes color. The old hairs simply fall out one by one and are replaced by hairs carrying the new color.

This fine covering of hair, fur, wool and hide, with its handsome and protective colors, has to be taken care of. An animal's life, as well as his comfort, may depend on how well he cleans himself.

Animal beauty parlor

An elephant likes and needs a daily bath. Without regular bathings the elephant's great hide would dry up and crack; parasitic insects might lay eggs in the cracks, causing the animal great torment if not illness. In the wild, an entire herd may often be seen bathing in a river or lake—sloshing through the shallows or sucking up water in their trunks to give themselves shower baths. In captivity, well-cared-for elephants are bathed twice a day, including a careful, all-over scrub. Lucky ones also get an occasional facial with cold cream.

One of the cleanest animals in the world is the wild pig. He keeps himself that way by bathing, not in water, but in mud or dust. He has no fur and his skin is very sparsely covered with stiff hairs called "bristles." Fleas or other biting pests could make life miserable

The Egyptian plover has a very dangerous-looking job—picking the teeth of the Nile crocodile.

Animal partnership: cattle egret eats the insect pests which the zebra stirs up as he walks.

for an animal with so little skin covering, so he takes pains to get rid of them. Wild pigs that live in damp areas make "wallows." Finding a muddy spot, the pig tramples around and through it, digging at it with his sharp hoofs, until he has a hollow of liquid mud. Then he lies down. The mud seeps through the bristles, cooling and cleaning the skin, and smothering any insects which might have taken up residence on his hide.

But bathing is not always necessary for cleanliness—not, at least, among animals equipped for dry cleaning.

The needle-clawed bush baby, a dis-

tant relative of the monkey, has a kind of built-in comb—a rigid piece of cartilage, edged by comb-like tiny teeth—growing under his regular tongue. It is used not only to comb the fur but to pick hair out of the animal's teeth. Most lemurs have lower teeth so arranged that they form an admirable comb.

The aye-aye, a peculiar kind of lemur, has one very thin and deft finger on each of his hands. He has several special uses for this finger. He taps on trees with it to detect the presence of insects, which he then eats. He drinks with it, scooping up water one drop at a time.

And he uses this special finger to comb and curry his fur. This is no small job. Although scarcely as big as a house cat, the aye-aye is covered with thick under wool and coarse guard hairs, and has an immense bushy tail, longer than his body.

Monkeys and apes spend hours currying one another. They comb through one another's fur with their fingernails, picking out the dirt they find. Most monkeys are insect eaters, and if one finds fleas or bugs in another's fur, he will eat them. But what they are really looking for is salt—or, rather, dry flakes of skin that taste like salt. (Human skin, too, tastes like salt; that is why a pet dog likes to lick his master's hand.)

Many rats and mice are meticulous combers and groomers. The little white-footed mouse, beset on all sides by a hundred enemies, nevertheless takes time to sit up and run his paws through his whiskers, rub his ears, scratch and clean his tiny body until he well deserves his name. When not out trading, courting, or cleaning house, the fastidious wood rat is probably engaged in grooming himself. The tiny European harvest mouse loves to bounce while he grooms; wrapping his grasping tail around a stalk of grass, he sways up and down in the wind while he busily washes his face and combs his fur.

Animals that spend much time in the water, particularly in cold climates, must take extra pains with their grooming. The beaver has two oil glands under his tail which keep his fur waterproof; in addition, there is a special combing claw on his hind foot for untangling and smoothing his guard hairs, which insulate him against cold.

And for certain lucky animals there are special cleaning services. The rhinoceros has an able and eager servant in the tick bird, which hops on his back to pluck parasites out of crevices and generally rid him of dirt and vermin. He also gives warning of danger with sharp cries. The Egyptian plover performs the same services for the Nile crocodile. He seems to have no fear at all of his formidable client, but walks in and out of the reptile's open mouth, probing between the teeth for leftover food.

Strange partnerships

Cattle egrets form partnerships with such animals as elephants, zebras, antelope, buffalo, sheep, cows and horses. The animal stirs up insects as he walks about and the bird eats them—and cattle ticks, which are a delicacy to egrets. The hippopotamus often has his teeth cleaned underwater by fish.

This is not social grooming, in which two members of the same species perform services for one another. This is "symbiosis" (mutual livelihood), a system by which two very *different* species benefit from living together and doing favors for one another.

The Animal Kingdom has many ways of getting necessary functions performed, even such everyday things as the bathing and the laundering.

101

CHAPTER

8

The Sense to Live

Some animals see better at night, others can't see at all. Some have no ears, and others—like snakes—smell with their tongues

102

In order to live and thrive, an animal must use good judgment. Taking in information and giving it out again—these two things are desperately important to all animals. To help them do it well, nature has blessed them with a wide variety of voices and sense organs and habits of life.

The first sense—the sense that most animals rely on to guide and inform them—is the sense of smell. A few good sniffs and an animal knows what is coming, from which direction, and probably why.

Many creatures navigate by smell. Salmon, for example, find their way back to their spawning places by means of scent. Ants, sometimes travelers over quite long distances, find their way to and from the colony by means of smell. It is also their primary means of recognizing one another.

In snakes, the organ of smell is located in the mouth, and the probe for this organ is the tongue. The "flickering tongue" of a snake, which sounds and looks so menacing, is the equivalent of the dog's sniffing nose.

Many animals have very sharp noses. An elephant's trunk—despite its being used for hauling lumber, spanking young, sucking up water, begging peanuts from zoo visitors, acting as a snor-

The cottontail makes a thumping noise with his hind foot to warn other rabbits: danger is near!

kel during river crossings, picking up small objects and performing many other functions—is first and foremost a nose, and a very good one, too. Downwind, an elephant can detect the presence of a man miles away. He can smell out water 10 feet underground—indeed, elephants are the water diviners of Africa, and in times of drought men sometimes follow them to take advantage of the wells they find and dig.

Mother mammals mark the identity of their young by licking them all over as soon as they are born. The little animal is then covered with his mother's smell and she and he officially belong together. The doe—mother deer—shows little affection for her fawn before he is licked. If an unlicked baby is removed from its mother, chances are she will not recognize it later as her own.

All-time champion smeller

But, of course, the champion smeller of all time is the dog and, among dogs, the hound—bloodhound, beagle, basset, foxhound, dachshund and many others. A good tracking dog can follow a trail that is forty-eight hours old. He can be given a shoe or necktie of the person to be traced and from that sample can pick out his man's trail.

Trackers are most commonly used in sport hunting, but they also do a great service in tracking down human beings. One famous bloodhound is credited with locating 2,500 lost persons.

There are many scent specialties.

Civet cats, musk-oxen, mink, many kinds of deer, peccaries, all are equipped with musk glands. Secretions from these glands are apparently used for attracting mates.

Other animals defend themselves with scent glands—not only the skunk, but the zoril of Africa and the teledu of Borneo and Sumatra. Both these animals are members of the weasel family, as is the skunk, and both enjoy virtual immunity from attack—lions are deathly afraid of the zoril.

Hearing—next-best protection

Next to smelling, hearing is probably the animal's most important sense. Sound acts as an alert, an attention-catcher, a direction-finder. For the hunted animal, hearing is probably his best protection.

Most reptiles and amphibians have excellent hearing—indeed, when Mr. Frog Goes A-Courtin', he relies primarily on the appeal of his voice to win his bride. Salamanders and snakes are believed to be deaf, although snakes quickly respond to vibrations. The celebrated "snake charming" of India is, of course, a staged performance: The snake rises from his basket when the lid is lifted and sways as his master sways—nervously keeping his head opposite the man's, so that he can strike if necessary.

Acute hearing is a necessity for a hunting animal. Aardvarks and pangolins listen at termites' nests for sounds of stirring within. If the nest has not been

The elephant's trunk is a very sensitive smelling organ. He can detect men miles off, can smell out water 10 feet underground—sometimes he can even locate water in a drought.

deserted, some faint sounds of life will catch the anteater's sharp ears. The aye-aye, of the lemur family, taps trees with his forefinger and then listens for insect sounds. Badgers stop at a mound to listen, in hopes of hearing the squeaks of baby moles.

In general, short, sharp, loud, crisp sounds are alarming to animals. Droning sounds, mumbles, singsongs, coos, humming tend to calm them down. Many cowboy songs were first invented as lullabies for nervous cattle that found this plaintive crooning very soothing.

Vision is probably much less impor-tant to most animals. Only to man, monkeys, apes and birds is it the foremost sense, and these are the very creatures that have the poorest senses of smell.

Many digging mammals either have no eyes at all, or their vision is so dim that it can be of little real protection. Many cave-dwelling snakes, fish, crayfish and lizards are completely eyeless—living in a world of night-and-day blackness, they have no need for eyes. Wolverines have rather poor sight; on the hunt they frequently sit up and shade their eyes with forepaws to get a better look at dinner possibilities.

105

As soon as her fawn is born, the mother doe licks him. This imparts her scent to him and establishes his identity. If he were not licked, she might not recognize the fawn later.

Most fish and amphibians have good vision at short range, usually within a limit of 3 feet. Brook fish sometimes leap out of the water to catch flying insects that are invisible to man. Turtles have good vision, and, being meat eaters, have need for sharp eyes. Crocodiles and alligators have fine vision, better at night than during the day. Their eyes are set high in their heads like periscopes, so that the animal can see even when nearly submerged.

Smelling, hearing, seeing—these tell an animal the important things about an object he encounters. But to fill in the details, he has other senses, some of them very specialized indeed.

The tastebuds of an octopus are located around the rims of his suckers—the many little suction cups with which his eight arms are lined. He tastes something by grasping it.

Fish are generously equipped with taste organs. Their nose openings consist of simple pits on the snout, lined with cells for smelling and tasting. In addition, some fish have small taste organs all over their bodies—they are like living tongues. So sensitive are the taste organs of some fish that they can detect the presence of food in a solution of 1 to 1,500,000—one drop of food to one and a half *million* drops of water.

To mammals, however, taste is a minor sense, used mainly to distinguish likes and dislikes.

Still, likes and dislikes are important to animal life. Often they determine where an animal will live, how far he will roam, what chances he will take in his food gathering. Orangutans love the fruit of the durian tree; although normally timid and shy of men, orangs will recklessly raid durian orchards, remain-

The wolverine shades his eyes to see better.

ing for days at a time within yards of a large village.

The shrew probably owes his continued existence to the fact that he isn't everybody's idea of a tasty meal. He is preyed upon by owls, snakes and some weasels, but dogs will not eat him, and neither will cats. In many areas he enjoys virtual immunity from attack simply because he doesn't taste very good.

Acutely sharp and delicate

The most primitive sense is that of touch. Even tiny, one-celled, microscopic creatures react when they are touched. In some animals, touch has been developed into an acutely sharp and delicate sense.

The mole lives by sense of touch. His eyes are small, able only to tell the difference between light and dark. His ears, though well developed, hear within a narrow frequency range. His sense of smell works efficiently only with nearby objects. But touch makes up for much of that.

Fingertips are excellent instruments of touch. The deft raccoon can feel out the mechanism of a lock or a garbage-can lid, can wipe the dirt off a pebble, can open doors or wiggle through a crack. His famous "washing" of food before eating it is left to his able fingers—the raccoon himself looks in every direction except at the food in his paws.

Monkeys, of course, use a sense of touch in many ways. In the wild, they probe into the crannies of trees hunting

107

for insects, test the strength of branches, clutch one another. In experiments with models substituted for real monkey mothers, it has been found that baby monkeys will choose a "soft" mother—one that feels right—in preference to one that merely gives them food.

An elephant has a great deal of dexterity in his "finger"—the triangular tip of his trunk—and can perform amazing movements with it. An elephant can grasp an orange or a blade of grass, a bale of hay or a puff of popcorn.

Despite his rather thick skin, an elephant is very sensitive to touch. He is ticklish and easily bothered by biting insects. Much as he loves water, he does not like water dripping on him slowly and incessantly, so he will leave forest areas during the rainy season.

An elephant's trunk is his most sensitive member. He curls it up out of the way whenever he feels it might become damaged or hurt, and in captivity he is most successfully punished by a smack across it. Hunters say that they can tell when an elephant really means to charge and when he is just bluffing by what he does with his trunk—if it is curled up out of harm's way, then watch out!

A time for every purpose

Almost all animals have a crude sense of time and season. Animals that hibernate know when the time has come to enter their burrows and sleep. Birds rise and sing at dawn, settle down for a few midday hours, rousing up again to feed and sing at sunset. All animals have seasons for mating and times for being abroad, night or day.

Perhaps the most remarkable sense of all those that animals possess is that of direction. An animal knows where he is. And without maps, without compasses, often without light, he also knows where he is going. Bats have a built-in sonar system. As they fly they give off little squeaks through their mouths—in some species, through their noses—and the echoes of these squeaks bounce off nearby objects and are caught by their extremely sharp ears. These little animals can tell, by the length of time it takes for the sound to echo back and the direction from which it comes, where the nearby objects are. This is called "echolocation"—steering by echo.

Feats of navigation

Bats are not the only animals with sonar. Many fish and insects are now thought to employ echolocation. Whales and dolphins make extensive use of it. Dolphins bleep and whistle at one another by way of "conversations," but when hunting fish they give off a steady creak. This creak travels underwater until it reaches a fish, then bounces off. The dolphin can tell from the echo where the fish can be found.

Other animal feats of navigation are on a longer-range scale. Dogs, for instance, are famous for finding their way home from great distances without a scent trail to follow. In a series of ex-

The octopus tastes with his tentacles. His taste organs are on the rims of his suckers.

periments, city dogs were released in strange neighborhoods miles from home and left to their own devices. Most found their way home eventually. The same dogs, released a second time in the same distant spot, streaked directly off for home, some inventing their own shortcuts.

Fur seals find their way to the tiny Pribilof Islands—yearling seals that have not seen the place since they left there with their mothers the previous spring. Sperm whales rendezvous in mid-ocean every year, and no one ever seems to take a wrong turning and end up somewhere else.

In addition to their receiving sets—the sense organs which take in information —animals are also equipped with sending devices. They can express their feelings to their fellows and to other animals by means of roars and chatters, with raps and with signal flags, in sound and in silence.

Fish grunt and groan; some species use sounds as a means of keeping the school together after dark. Frogs buzz, croak, whirr, all in an effort to summon and court their mates. And alligators bellow, setting the swamps to reverberating with their noise.

The most persistent of animals, as well as the most colorful, are the birds. In the spring they sing, and the rest of the year they call, and few of them are silent for very long at a time.

109

Birds can achieve a wide variety of meanings in the sounds they make. Jackdaws make a wild rattling noise when a cat appears. Appearance of a bird enemy sends the blue jay flying through the woods to caw an advance warning. Migrating geese honk at each other regularly while in flight, presumably giving signals.

For sheer variety of sound—in volume, in pitch, in quality of tone—the mammals are hard to beat. They do not cry out so often as birds do, but when they do make sounds they are apt to be impressive ones.

Lions and tigers roar, of course—everybody knows that. So do leopards, jaguars and ounces (snow leopards). These five are the "great cats"—so-called not because of their size but because they can roar. Pumas scream, lynxes and bobcats yowl, house cats caterwaul—when we hear a roar, we know it is a big fellow.

Yelps, yaps, howls and whistles

And not all members of the dog family howl. The dingo yelps, the fox yaps, the dhole has a curious whistling cry, the Cape hunting dog barks and yelps, the bush dog of South America whimpers, the jackal wails. But the wolf howls—indeed, his famous howl, answered by others of his pack, has sent shudders down human spines for hundreds of years. When it comes to bloodcurdling sounds, however, the hyena stands alone. He can howl and yelp and

The raccoon washes his food with slim, deft fingers. He has a delicate sense of touch.

growl as well as any other animal, but when he is approaching a meal—often the carcass of an animal that has simply dropped dead—he produces a sound like a laugh. It is a wild, rattling cackle, described as "insane," which carries for long distances and is quite unlike the cry of any other animal.

Many animals have special cries for warning. A colony of prairie dogs is enjoying the morning sun, each animal sitting at the entrance to his burrow. One dog spots an enemy and gives a shrill warning yap. Like a flash, everyone dives down into his hole.

There are other animal sounds of special meaning. Mothers often have a sound which they use only for their young. Sometimes there is one note for soothing and another for scolding, perhaps even a third for calling them back when they stray off.

Mammals of the sea are often fond of making a racket. Belugas and narwhals are considered the noisiest of whales. Traveling in great pods (whale herds), they sport in the Arctic water, mooing at one another, giving Bronx cheers, whistling.

Animals have other means of expressing themselves besides their vocal cords. The beaver slaps the water with his tail as he dives. This is not necessarily a danger signal, but it catches the attention of the other beavers working nearby; they can then take a quick look around to see what made their comrade take to the water.

The cottontail thumps with his hind foot when danger threatens. So does the rock wallaby, a small kangaroo. So does the wood rat; he also taps on dry leaves with his tail—both noises carry for a considerable distance. The white-footed mouse drums on hollow reeds. The

A prairie dog's special whistle signals danger. Hearing it, an entire colony dives below.

The beaver makes a loud, whacking sound by slapping his broad, flat tail on the water. In times of danger, this alerts other beavers—and sometimes other kinds of animals as well.

brush-tailed porcupine of Africa carries a dry rattle in his tail, as does the rattlesnake.

Animals can also communicate in silence—often over quite long distances. Most famous for this is the pronghorn, an American "antelope." He has a rump patch of white hairs that stand erect when the muscles of the skin contract. In a moment of danger, the animal tenses up, and the white hairs rise and spread, like a white signal flag opening out. It can be seen 2 to 4 miles away on level ground and instantly alerts other pronghorns in the neighborhood.

Gestures or movements are often highly suggestive to animals. Among stags, standing up on the hind legs expresses aggression and invites attack. One stag, sharing a zoo enclosure with a kangaroo, attacked his roommate whenever the poor kangaroo sat back on his tail.

Taken as a whole, no other family of animals can express itself vocally as does the tribe of monkeys and apes. Sound is important to them—and sound is what they make plenty of.

All gibbons howl a good bit, but none can touch the siamang of Sumatra. He is only 3 feet tall when standing erect and has pipe-cleaner-thin arms and legs and a narrow body. But when he lets go with a morning whoop, this scrawny creature can compete successfully with a trumpeting elephant in full voice.

The siamang's only close rival at sound production is his distant cousin on the other side of the world, the howler monkey of South America. So powerful is this voice that one individual can sound like an entire tribe with no trouble at all.

All members of the monkey family seem to produce a wide variety of noises, and many studies are under way to determine how much meaning one animal can communicate to another purely by sound. Already men have made a beginning at "translating" a number of monkey "languages." Perhaps some day man will be able to "speak monkey."

In experiments with marmosets, men have found that the sound that means "I want water" is quite different from the sound meaning "I want milk." Marmosets have a variety of alarm calls, and it is claimed that their cry for "Watch it! A black cat!" is detectably different from "Watch it! A white cat!" Moreover, in addition to these and an enormous variety of gibbers and chatters that we know marmosets indulge in, it is also possible that their "language" is partly supersonic—too high for human hearing—like that of dolphins.

Chimpanzee vocabulary

Chimpanzees still lead the parade, however. Experimenters have noted that laboratory chimps are capable of producing thirty-two different sounds, mostly explosive grunts. Other observers report that wild chimpanzees plainly influence one another with the sounds they make. One old male, having made friends with his observer, used to walk up beside her, and say in greeting, "Hoo."

One male howling monkey in full voice can make noise that sounds like a whole troop.

CHAPTER

9

Louder Than Words

What jumps 60 feet? What bird flies 95 miles an hour? What catches its dinner in mid-air? What cat swims with real delight?

Most members of the Animal Kingdom are true creatures of habit. Many, indeed, are creatures of instinct, for the ways of life which they follow were inherited from their parents, along with their eyesight, their skin covering, and the structure of their bodies.

But some animals have far more to them than that. Men are only now begining to appreciate animal intelligence, animal strength, animal courage—and animal charm. Actions speak louder than words in explaining animal ways.

Most animals specialize in their talents and abilities. These have such a wide range that there is hardly any field in which some animal does not excel.

Over short distances, many animals can attain astounding speeds: the cheetah, 70 miles per hour; the pronghorn and the springbuck, 60; the lion, 50; the antelope jack rabbit, 45.

There are great leapers in the Animal Kingdom, too. The tree-living kangaroo has been known to jump down—from the limb to the ground—a full 60 feet, the height of a five-story building. Pumas can jump up—from the ground to a rock ledge—12 to 15 feet. The great gray kangaroo performs the greatest high jumps—9 feet is the record height.

The flight of many birds and insects has been timed. The racing pigeon can

The great gray kangaroo bounds on his hind feet only and uses his heavy tail to keep his balance.

The cheetah is the fastest of all in the Animal Kingdom. He can clock as much as 70 miles per hour—over short distances only. With more ground to cover, even he must slow down.

fly at 95 miles per hour; the canvasback duck, 72; the merlin falcon, 55. Dragonflies—tiny things only 3 inches long—can do 55 m.p.h.; bumblebees 35; honeybees, 20; grasshoppers, 15.

As for diving speeds, a peregrine falcon can probably drop on his prey at a speed of 200 m.p.h. or more.

Digging is another field of endeavor at which some animals excel. The echidna or spiny anteater can bury himself in ten minutes and then keep ahead of a human being trying to dig him out. In light soil, a mole can dig a foot a minute. The aardvark digs himself burrows

so large that a small man can stand up in them.

Animal strength is a difficult thing to measure, but there are some amazing feats on record. One giant pangolin can win a tug-of-war with ten full-grown men and one gorilla can do the same with fifteen—and by using only one hand, too.

The pangolin can raise up almost anything at all, provided he can get his nose under it. The otter, another with a strong nose, can pry apart any two things he can get his muzzle between. The coendou, a South and Central

American porcupine, can gnaw his way out of almost any wooden crate overnight. The cutting grass, a cane rat of West Africa, can chew a hole in a corrugated iron fence. A pair of giant armadillos once dug their way out of a pit made of concrete 1 foot thick.

Animal athletes

The weasel can kill an animal nearly a hundred times his own size. A grizzly can lop off a 4-inch-thick tree with one swipe of his paw. The charge of an elephant or a rhinoceros can derail a train —and has, a number of times.

Some animals specialize in agility. Deft of foot are the wild goats and sheep native to mountain regions throughout the world. The chamois of the Alps is probably the best known of these athletic beasts, famous for his wild leaps from crag to crag. He has cup-shaped hollows on the under sides of his hoofs, and these act like suction cups, helping him to cling to the smallest of footholds. The bighorn sheep of North America goes him one better by leaping off 150-foot cliffs, and breaking his fall by bouncing off the cliff face at intervals all the way down.

Other animals are deft of mouth or nose. Wild pigs, with their sharp wits and agile snouts, are masters of all sorts of tricks. In captivity, they quickly learn how to reach through the bars and lift the latch.

Nimble fingers serve an animal superlatively well—and never better than

The peregrine falcon is justly famed for his diving speed—estimated at 200 m.p.h.

when some human being thinks he has the creature well caged. The raccoon is a master at lifting hooks and untwisting wire and, in other ingenious ways, poking and prying his way to freedom.

True masters of the art of escape, however, are the monkeys and apes with the combination of bright, inquisitive minds and tireless fingers. Among monkeys and apes, the all-time star, the Harry Houdini of the Animal Kingdom, is the orangutan. An orangutan likes to keep busy, and he is deft, ingenious and strong. Even a baby orang can dismantle a traveling cage, unless it is specially

117

The daredevil chamois is the athlete of the Alps, leaping from one crag to another.

reinforced and kept under strict watch. An adult orang can pull trapezes from their concrete moorings, unbolt shelves used for sleeping, pick metal labels off the front of his cage—all apparently in an artless search for entertainment and enlightenment. To an orangutan, a cage is not so much a container as a plaything.

"Millionaires" of the Animal Kingdom

How intelligent are animals? Nobody can say for sure, but there have been some educated guesses. Apes and monkeys, it is believed, are capable of true reasoning. This means that confronted with a problem they have never faced before they can reason out a solution. In the wild they make crude tools, such as stripping twigs from sticks to dig with or forming leaves into drinking cups. In captivity, they have learned to "work" for "money"—by pulling a lever, they earn a poker chip, which can be dropped into a slot to produce food or water or a piggyback ride. Some laboratory chimps have turned into regular little misers, hoarding their hard-earned poker chips instead of squandering them and often lording it over other chimps that are not so "rich."

Men who have studied the dolphin have a high opinion of this animal's intelligence. The bottle-nose can learn to do something by demonstration—being shown how three or four times—a thing monkeys cannot do (but apes can). He masters tricks easily and invents variations of his own. In experiments in

Chimpanzees have the highest I.Q. in the Animal Kingdom. They even make and use tools.

learning, he catches the point with amazing speed. Despite his lack of hands, despite his mode of life in a totally strange element, despite all the ways in which he is different from men, he has maintained a friendship for human beings since ancient days. Perhaps intelligence is the basis for it.

Elephants are also highly intelligent creatures. There are many instances of elephants solving new problems. Furthermore, they are the only draft animals that can be trained to do more than simply pull or carry. In Burmese lumbering camps, they handle heavy teak logs, dragging them, stacking them, sending them down chutes, straightening them out when they jam. They help train young elephants and punish naughty adult ones and capture wild ones. They can be trained for hunting or load carrying or circus performing.

The elephant is the only animal that can stand on his head. He can be guided by voice instructions by those who know him. He frequently has nightmares. He has a sense of humor, too, say those who know him well, and will play jokes if he has the chance.

But does the elephant forget? Frequently, say his trainers—things go in one great big ear and out the other. But once he has mastered a trick or a chore or a face or the sound of a voice—then he never forgets it.

Which animal is the longest-lived? Sturgeon are thought to reach the age of 80, halibut the age of 60. A toad that escapes being killed may eventually pass his thirtieth birthday. The great tortoises of the Galápagos Islands are believed to live 150 years or more, making them the Methuselahs of the reptile class. Parrots live to be 80 or more and ravens to 70. But among mammals, the longest-lived is clearly man.

Animal old age

Records of 105, 110, and 115 years of age for man have been fairly well established. Old age usually does not even begin until age 65 or 70, and many vigorous people are still active at 80. Man far outlives his nearest mammal rivals.

Elephants probably come closest, with a recorded age limit of 69. In the wild, Asiatic elephants are said to live to 80 or more and African elephants to 100 or more, but these are only expert estimates. Other animals rarely live beyond 50. The hippo, great Indian rhino, finner whale, echidna, chacma baboon and chimpanzee all have life spans in the 40s. Lions, pygmy hippos, wild bears, horses and zebras can live to be 30 plus. Giraffes, wombats, seals, hyenas, kinkajous, small dogs, cats, goats and certain bats are long-lived at 20. Most small mammals rarely see their tenth birthday and many do not live to be 5.

What creatures survive best? Mainly those which reproduce fast—like rodents, hedgehogs, and moles—and those which adapt to change—domesticated animals and pets, and wild carnivores.

Bears are adaptive animals. They will eat almost anything and live almost anywhere. They take to zoo life with gusto and survive in captivity for thirty years or more. In national parks, black bears quickly learn when and where to beg for food, and how to rob a camper's store of food. In Eastern woods, too, they are becoming insufferably bold.

Rats are adaptable animals. So are hyenas, opossums, foxes, skunks, baboons, mice and many others. The raccoon is fast learning to neglect hunting in favor of raiding garbage dumps and fields of sweet corn. The gray squirrel, once a forest animal, has adapted so well to the coming of cities that he can hardly live without begging. House cats alternately prowl back fences and curl up to sleep on top of the family TV set —taking the best of both worlds. All these animals have survived persecution and are doing just fine.

Old wives' tales

Men are slowly getting to know the members of the Animal Kingdom a little better. They are making more careful observation of animal life and slowly discarding many myths and false beliefs.

Whales and dolphins are, as a rule, marine (salt-water) animals. However, beluga whales swim 600 miles up the Yukon River and pilot whales are frequently seen in bays and estuaries. There are at least four species of dolphin which are permanently freshwater. Seals, too, are marine animals, but there are seal populations in the Cas-

Unlike humans, penguins are not at all anxious to be first into the water. Unseen danger may be waiting. So they shove and crowd at the water's edge until one finally falls in.

pian Sea and in Lake Baikal in Russia.

Despite their skill at navigation and echolocation, whales frequently run aground. It is sure death for the whale when this happens, for his lungs may soon become crushed by his own great weight, and he suffocates. And yet many grounded whales, when towed out to sea, return directly to shore and run aground again. Such creatures usually turn out to be suffering from diseases of some kind, often infected lungs, and it may be that the animal is trying to find a way to breathe more easily.

On the other hand, sometimes whole pods of whales run aground. Usually these are pilot whales, which follow their leader quite blindly and make a habit of swimming offshore. But it has also happened with sperm whales, the deepest swimming of all whales. Nobody has ever explained this curious behavior.

Some whales are easily frightened of men. Frogmen, feeding and playing with the belugas at the New York Aquarium, must enter the tank one at a time. On the other hand, wild pilot whales will frolic in bays and estuaries, apparently unafraid of human spectators, while wild porpoises are credited with saving human lives, and wild

121

dolphins have frequently been tamed. Pelorus Jack, a member of a species called "Risso's dolphin," became famous in New Zealand around the turn of the century; for ten years or more, the animal acted as self-appointed convoy for steamers crossing Cook Strait between the cities of Nelson and Wellington.

Fun with humans

Sea lions, it is said, enjoy romping in the water with human beings. Even in the wild, they have very little fear of man, and can often be closely approached.

Penguins love water, of course, but a group of them will push and struggle *not* to be the first one in—there may be leopard seals, their arch foe, in the water, and no one wants to be the one to find out for sure.

Tigers are not really "at home" in the jungle. The tiger was originally a mountain animal (some tigers still do inhabit hill country) and suffer greatly from tropical heat. That is why he goes swimming regularly, apparently for pleasure. He is not the only cat who likes water, either. The jaguar is a strong swimmer and spends a good deal of his time in the water, often simply playing. The fishing cat of India and Burma, a 3-foot-long creature with gray fur and black spots, lives in marshy areas and eats almost nothing but fish.

The tiger can jump around corners—turn his body in a different direction in mid-leap. The mighty lion, however, must leap the way he aims himself. Unlike the agile tiger, the lion can be easily sidestepped.

Gorillas, for all their immense strength and forbidding looks, are by nature shy and retiring creatures. In the wild, they usually duck when they see men coming or use the bushes as shields. Sometimes they will rise up and "display," pounding their chests in warning to the intruders. In rare instances, they will attack. In zoos, they have proved themselves tidy, quiet, clean and affectionate beasts—perfect gentlemen when compared with the rowdy chimpanzees and the inquisitive orangs.

The human mental image of a snake as a relentless and evil enemy is very one-sided. Pythons have a fearsome reputation, but they are the favorites of circus snake dancers, because they are so gentle. The krait, an exceedingly venomous relative of the cobra, kills more people than any other snake in his native India. But he is nocturnal and very sensitive to light—so sensitive that in bright daylight he is often unable to strike or even to move at all.

In contrast, hummingbirds can be ferocious little creatures. The males often fight one another, using their long beaks as stabbing weapons. Fortunately, under their brilliant, flashing plumage they have exceedingly tough hides. They apparently fear no other creature on earth, not even man.

It was once believed that flies could not feel emotion, only sensations such as

122

The tiger is not a water-hating cat. He suffers from the heat, goes swimming to cool off.

heat, cold, light, darkness. But it is now believed that many insects know fear, and hate and love—at least in a primitive way.

Ant colonies carry on extensive trading in food, it has been found. One colony will trade only with another colony of the same species. Bees maintain a central distribution center for nectar. Worker bees bring their supplies into the center of the hive where the queen is. From there it is parceled out to other parts of the colony.

One thing that can be counted on

Actually, there is only one thing about animals that can always be counted on: They are unpredictable. Even men who know them best are regularly surprised and outwitted.

Malayan tapirs are normally the most gentle and harmless of beasts, but when their anger is aroused, they can do terrible damage, rasping with the undersides of their snouts. Frank Buck—the animal collector who was accustomed to handling tigers and leopards with cool professionalism—was once nearly killed by a tapir.

Beavers are considered stolid, unthinking animals, merely following blind instinct when they build their elaborate dams and ledges and canals. But the New York Zoological Society once acquired a pair of beavers and put them in an enclosure built with all the things beavers seem to like. There was a running stream, just the right size and

The archerfish wings his insect dinner by spitting out well-aimed pellets of water.

pressure of water. There were building materials, tree trunks and branches and stones and clay and leaves. But the beavers did not build a dam—they built a ramp up the wall of the enclosure, and if their keeper had returned half an hour later the following morning, they would have made a successful zoo break.

Ringtailed lemurs of Madagascar and meercats of South Africa—both animals from dry and rocky homelands—love shower baths; in captivity, they will spend hours under a dripping faucet. The spotted skunk likes to walk on his hands; sometimes this means he is about to squirt, but more often it is simply his idea of fun.

Some birds enjoy covering themselves with ants or taking a dust bath on an anthill. This is called "bird anting." Apparently the formic acid on the ants' bodies and in the hill dust feels good on the birds' skins. Other birds "ant" with lemon juice or moth balls.

Elephants are often terrified of airplanes, but an elephant will usually allow himself to be loaded aboard, and will remain quiet during the flight, if he has a chicken perched on his head.

Man is not the only animal who gets drunk. When an elephant herd finds a grove of fermented fruit, the animals become quite uproarious, bellowing and reeling in great good humor. (A few teetotalers, of course, withdraw from the others and glare in disapproval at their wayward brethren.) In Africa, fruit bats sometimes drink the palm sap that has been drawn off from trees and left to ferment; the poor bats become so besotted, they fall from their perches in a stupor.

The camel has always expressed his contempt for man by spitting in his face —usually an evil-smelling mess of half-chewed vegetation. His cousins, the llama, alpaca and vicuña, do the same thing, with gravel for ammunition.

A much daintier spitter is the little archerfish of Southeastern Asia, which brings down flies and other insects of the air by hitting them with drops of water. One group of archerfish, kept as pets by a Siamese scholar, used to attract their master's attention by spitting out his cigarette.

But perhaps the most maddening and amazing animals of all are those supposedly docile and domesticated creatures, the sheep. At the Cornell University Experimental Station, a special maze was built just for sheep, with blind alleys and many choices and, at the end, a reward of food. The purpose of the experiment was to see how quickly the sheep could learn all the turnings and so reach the reward.

But the experiment failed. Rats run through mazes to get rewards. So do cats, dogs, mice, insects and even earthworms. But apparently not sheep.

The Cornell sheep were not interested in the reward, they were interested in the maze. They wouldn't dream of leaving it. Turned out of their barns in the morning, they raced to the entrance of the maze, pushing and shoving to be first. Then, when one was selected, she strolled in through the gate—and there she stayed. The Cornell men finally got tired of watching a sheep recline at her ease in the midst of a maze and gave up the experiment. People still do not know how bright sheep are—maybe it is better if they don't know.

Sheep, elephants, pythons, porpoises, man, prairie dogs, seals, flamingos, alligators—hundreds of thousands of kinds of creatures share the globe. They have habits in common and habits not in common, and all of them are interesting.

125